TALKS
WITH
JONATHON

Book I
A Guide to Transformation

As told to
ROBIN MILLER

Library of Congress Cataloging-in-Publication Data
93-073043
1. Channeling 2. Metaphysical 3. Psychic
4. Personal Transformation 5. Spirit Communication

ISBN 1-881343-04-9

Published by

Channel One
Communications, Inc.
30 Pleasant Street, Needham, MA 02192

Printed by
MISSION POSSIBLE PRINTING
P.O. Box 1495 • Sedona, AZ 86339 • (602) 282-6523

INTRODUCTION

My first connection with the being who calls himself Jonathon began January 23, 1991. I awoke early in the morning from a dream in which I was being taught and spoken to about my life and direction. As I awoke, I was repeating certain thoughts aloud, and when I became fully conscious, I decided that I should write down the phrases and thoughts that I recalled.

When I sat down to remember and write, I found that I was tapping into thoughts that were not my own, and the pen moved effortlessly from thought to thought without my direction and interaction. After reading what had just come through me, I was astonished, not only by the concepts which I had not related but also by the ease of the process itself. The correlation of thought from sentence structure to paragraph ideas intrigued me for it all seemed to make sense on a deeper level as well as being concise in the formation of ideas.

I found that I was being called upon to write in this manner at every given opportunity, and I allowed the process to unfold and the bonding with the entity to become stronger. As we continued in this way, I realized that, over time, not only did the process itself become easier but I was also experiencing changes and transformation within my own being and thought processes. I became more open, compassionate, loving, and tolerant of all life and experiences, seeing the positive, hopeful side of things instead of the negative side. I found I was becoming more and more receptive to inner messages and spiritual insights. Magic seemed to come alive all around me and within me. The world and my perceptions of it based on limited beliefs seemed to expand and take on new meaning as the blending of energies between Jonathon and me grew.

I feel a wondrous surge of aliveness even now as I write when I inwardly connect with the vibration of his Love and wisdom. Truly, never before has a being touched me like this one nor has one reached into the depths of my soul to guide me through inspiration and understanding of my life's greater purpose.

I am a musician, songwriter, and poet who has dabbled in art, philosophy, and metaphysics. I have meditated, prayed, om'd, and done all of the many things one does when looking for answers and truth in the search for life's meaning. Yet, in all of my 41 years, I have never been as moved, altered, and loved as I am now and have been since this interaction began with Jonathon. Whatever happens with this information or its outcome is truly not as important to me personally as are the guidance, Love, and wonderful knowingness that he not only exists, but that he is here for me and for all who call upon him. The experience of the connection to higher levels of being is completely beyond compare and description. As with all things in life, this must be experienced for oneself. One cannot convince another of the truth or validity of such experiences; one can only view the effects and changes within the personality and life of the one blessed by it.

I Love this being with all my heart and soul for he has been and continues to be a blessing of Love, guidance, and wisdom in my life. As you share in my experience, may you hear and connect with those ideas of Love, trust, and truth which Jonathon offers freely to all.

In this day and age of the explosion of consciousness, there are many people such as me who are making this connection with higher energies of Light and wisdom. When I asked Jonathon, "Why me?" he simply stated that I was to add my voice to the Divine choir of awakening beings and spread the message of God's Love and Light. That purpose is being fulfilled here and now by the publication of his thoughts and ideas and loving wisdom. May all who read these words come away a little Lighter, more uplifted in hope and faith, and carrying with them the thought that they are truly loved more than they know, now and always.

I dedicate this book to Jonathon and the Brotherhood of Light and to all who read and identify within their souls with the message they bring. May we all come to know and realize our own God-self and thereby hasten in the New Age of Spirit with Love and gentleness in our hearts.

Robin Miller
Sedona, Arizona
February 9, 1991

ACKNOWLEDGEMENTS

I would like to thank the following people for their guidance and help in seeing this work to completion:

Sonia Martin, for her expertise in transcribing and editing this book. Without her talents, Jonathon's words would still be in Middle English as they were given to me. She helped convince me that present-day readers would probably appreciate modern English much more, and after seeing the final product, I heartily agree.

I would also like to lovingly thank my mate, Helen, who was there in the beginning of my initial contact with Jonathon and who helped convince me that I wasn't losing my mind as his words and thoughts came through me; for her unwavering support through all my changes, and for her loving understanding that has been a catalyst for all the many transitions in the three years since Jonathon has come into our lives.

I also wish to thank my children, Tiffany, Eric, and Jason, for being my greatest teachers; my dear friends and supporters, Rion, Joumana, and Maya, for their wisdom and Love; and to all the many wonderful friends who have come into my life since I moved to Sedona, Arizona.

Also, my gratitude to Richard Satterfield of Channel One Communications, Inc., my publisher, for believing in and taking a chance on the first of a series of five works by Jonathon.

And, finally, I give many thanks and blessings to the being who made it all possible, Jonathon; for his patience with me all the times I doubted and struggled with the validity of my experience; for his wisdom in knowing my fears and helping me push through them; and for his selfless Love which he so freely bestows through his thoughts, words, and actions.

My hope is that his words are received in the Love in which they were bestowed, and that each individual is moved to a deeper awareness of their own Divine Light and God-self.

Blessings.

TALKS WITH JONATHON

BOOK I

A Guide to Transformation
As Told To
ROBIN MILLER

PREFACE

The message I bring is one of hope, love and the foreverness of your being, the ongoingness of life. Within the shadows of your fears there is joy awaiting through your own recognition of truth. And what is that truth? Simply that all of Creation within all dimensions and planes of being are one, forever united in Love and laughter; that you and I are children of Light, children of Spirit, dancing and frolicking in the universal plan of Divine eternalness; and that which transpires within this great and wondrous plan is now, in this momentous moment, your own awakening. The dream, the illusion of eons of false belief in your own separation, is almost at an end. Your limited past perception of that which is real and that which is unreal is soon to be altered as your hearts and minds expand to greater understanding of your place within the perfect order of cosmic awareness. Awaken, oh Humanity, behold your Godself. Behold the unlimited Light, the eternal Love that you are. Behold and walk in joy, freedom, and bliss. Behold *yourself*, oh Humanity.

I am

Jonathon of the Seventh Ray,

Speaker of the Council for the Brotherhood of Light

CONTENTS

I

✦

I Am Jonathon

✦

I am Jonathon, a being such as yourself, who has walked many miles and experienced many lifetimes in form within your physical plane of being. I have been born, and I have died; I have felt pleasure and pain, joy and sorrow within third-dimensional existence. I fully understand and empathize with the human plight within the denseness of this Earth school. I have grown and suffered through the desires of the flesh more times than I care to say, and I am here to report that there is hope, there is Light waiting in the wings upon the stage of your life and times, and the awakening of Humanity into higher, fourth-dimensional understanding is imminent! Be prepared, therefore, as I speak to you of that which is, that which is to come, and the emergence of God-Spirit into your hearts and minds.

I have retained the name "Jonathon" for it fits the vibration of my beingness as well as being the name I held upon my last and final incarnation upon your plane, Terra. Although the spirit of my being is sexless, even as your own is in greater formlessness, I retain the masculine principle for purposes of identification and individual vibration.

Now, that which I and those beings who work with me seek to convey and impart is the foreverness of your being and the knowledge of infinite Love which sustains and supports your soul within the God-Force Principle. I am part of a group of seven entities who work together with many other groups and organizations of Light for the direct purpose of reawakening mankind to his true purpose, his true God-self connection. We move and traverse through various levels and sublevels of reality and vibrational structure, weaving our web of Light within the hearts and minds of those who are now or who in the future will be ready and willing and desirous of our connection. That which we have to offer is simple: a new way of perceiving the being called "self"! It is a revolutionary concept of becoming that which you truly are: God-Force Principle!

We work both individually and collectively to access and transform cellular and subcellular patterns of thought and behavior concepts, thereby allowing openings of unlimitedness to filter into conscious awareness and facilitate awakening of the individual to his own highest God-self. Our presence is felt only by those whose desire and determination for greater understanding and unfoldment is requested, for we never push our way into consciousness unless one is ready, willing, and open for the connection.

We are known as the "Brotherhood of Light," and are ever working with other groups such as the Great White Brotherhood, the Great Golden Seal, the Celestial Hierarchy of Light, the Ashtar Command, the Angelic Forces, Jesus, the Christed One, the Enlightened Buddha, bodhisattvas, and various saints, sages, and interdimensional as well as extradimensional entities of Love, Light, and Wisdom. Our forces are great and growing daily as others awaken to the greater Light of knowingness of their own divinity within God.

Upon Terra now there are an unprecedented number of Light beings incarnating into form in the united tasks of awakening Humanity to its own illumination within form. There is a Divine "push" for the collective, harmonious enlightenment to occur for there is little time left in your dimension as you know and understand time. The energies of Light and awakening are ever increasing and enfolding your planet and all dimensions. Those greater forces are being accelerated on every level of experience, moment to moment.

The necessity to align yourself and your vibration with this influx of higher frequency is all-important and is a large part of our purpose in this communication with you now. We shall impart to you methods and practices for your evolving acceleration of frequency that shall ease your transition as these energies increase even more in the months and years to come. Your planet and schoolroom of Terra is greatly loved and held in the highest honor and respect by those of us who were incarnate upon her wondrous planetary body and part of her "curriculum."

All those of my group were part of her history and karmic wheel of rebirth before graduation through cosmic union with the God-Force Principle of our own beings. We, too, walked in darkness and struggle from lifetime to lifetime upon her ground and felt the pain of sorrow, destruction, and death. We, too, dealt with all the issues, the confusion, and the despair that all Humanity shares as it strives in the nighttime of its search for self-understanding.

Within us all came that momentous time, that sublime, wordless occasion when, from eons of experience, self-doubt, and hatred, we let go of all the beliefs, fears, and thoughts of self-limitation and jumped from the mountain of ego attachment. In that moment, instead of oblivion, came Light! It was the Light of a thousand suns, the Light of a thousand lives, the Light of understanding, the Light of joy, the Light of God-self! In that moment, we realized ourselves to be not mortal, frail human beings but formless Spirit and endless joy, experiencing God's dream through third-dimensional living.

And when it came upon us, there was no warning, no expectation; yet, the timelessness of the experience of cosmic awakening released us from the bonds of Earth and broke the chains of the cycle of rebirth onto this plane of vibratory experience. We are here to relate to you the joys to be found within your being, the access to your wisdom through self-love, and this personal expansion into impersonal God union.

That is our goal, our purpose, our task, and the united collective task of all who work toward Humanity's rebirth into Light. As we operate in realms of being quite unknown to you, we quietly implant messages of hope, faith, trust, Light, and laughter into your awareness in hopes that in those moments of openness, our presence will be felt and acknowledged. When another of your race becomes receptive through the allowance of trust and letting go of those rigid belief patterns of thought which restrict consciousness, we rejoice in his opening and flood his being with our Light and understanding, giving unto his consciousness only that which he is ready to receive and process within concepts of thought and mental vibration. As he opens more, we give him yet more to "chew on," so to speak, and in his process of unfoldment not only to the reception of subtle energies which we are imparting to him, but within his own personal path of enlightenment as well. As we increase our connection with him, his frequency of cellular and subcellular vibration is quickened. Through that quickening comes even greater spiritual understanding and insight upon his consciousness until that time when he, too, may "let go and let God," thereby experiencing the "Cosmic Kiss" of "the peace which passeth understanding." Within that enlightening moment, his own freedom is decreed, for he is now liberated from the karmic consequences of past lives and is freed from rebirth into form. That experience, once known, is the greatest, the most joyous, Light-filled, kingdom-of-heaven consciousness one can experience while in physical form. No other desire and fulfillment of it can come close to the awesomeness, the indescribable bliss of your soul's reunion with God in consciousness.

That is the goal, the prize, the pot of gold at the end of the rainbow of your experience within physical form. Once attained, all your lifetimes, all your experiences are seen for what they truly are: your own dream.

It is time, oh Humanity, to awaken from your self-created dream and walk united in the Light of your own God-self!

It is the dawn of your Father's entry into form and the awareness of his purpose and destiny for all!

It is a new day for mankind in which he shall look upon his brother and see himself behind his brother's eyes: one in Spirit and harmony.

It is the day of the Lord on Earth, and you are part of the Greater Plan of Awakening.

Oh Humanity, awaken!

Take up your sword of Truth and Light and do battle with the forces of lower thought-forms of self-doubt and fear and become the victor of your limited perception.

Oh Humanity, awaken!

May the Divine Light of the Father's Infinite Love guide you and your brothers ever onward and inward to the source of your bliss, your Light, your knowing.

Om. Peace. Bliss. Understanding!

I am Jonathon, Speaker of the Council for the Brotherhood of Light.

Talks With Jonathon

II

♦

The Oneness of
Spirit and the
Many Mansions of
God's Infinite
Being

♦

Within the Infinite Mind of God's eternal thought, you and I and all living life forms in all worlds and dimensions of being have their existence. Throughout the endless universe of form and nonform, all is held within that omnipresent thought, and that thought is called Love.

The very pattern and structure of the atoms and molecules which make up your human body are held together with that same vibration of Love. All of Creation is connected in likeness of being and unity of Spirit even though various forms are perceived as individual and distinct; yet, all are interwoven and intricately connected on finer levels of Spirit oneness. In other words, all that you perceive, although seemingly separate and having individual existence within greater perceptiveness, is known to be part of you and all of Creation. The ocean is you, the sky is you, your enemy is you, and so on within the framework of the law and harmony of God's Infinite Being. We are all one! This is the "Law of the Divinity of All" and the eternal presence within all of Creation; it always has been and ever shall be! Your own divinity, though unknown to mortal man's consciousness, is the gift of the Father-God Principle to all thought creation.

Within the Infinite Mind are endless levels of vibratory Creation, each being "home" to that like vibratory level held by an individual's thought consciousness. There are as many mansions of God's being as there are individual, evolving conscious thoughts of the Creator. There are an infinite number of thoughts within the mind of God. Yet, within the infinity of the Father's kingdom, all is with harmony and proper placement according to evolutionary Spirit consciousness and self-awareness. The finest mind and intellect cannot possibly fathom the immensity of God's order within the cosmos of Spirit evolution and the cycle therein. Only the consciousness expanded into God's heavenly realm can hope to glimpse the vast beauty, Love, and harmony which is shared and owned by all of God's Creation.

The mind purified by enlightenment of Spirit's purpose within the "Law of All" is the key to the door which, when once opened, shall never be closed again to your consciousness. Within the Divine Law of Vibration there exists separation only within the level of consciousness expanse and the degree therein. Therefore, within your own level of vibrating consciousness, for example, although countless dimensions of life and consciousness could exist and are existing all around and within your field of beingness, you are not aware of or within perception of these for they vibrate at greater, finer frequencies and are therefore imperceptible to you at this time. As you advance and raise your own frequency rate, however, you shall be able to sense and feel their presence about your vibrational field, depending on your sensitivity to the subtle variations of vibration.

Therefore, "God's many mansions" are held intact within His thoughts through the power of His Love and Infinite Mind. All life is supported in the same fashion, sustaining throughout all the vast universes of form and nonform, endlessly, ever alive, ever evolving higher and higher back to the oneness of being within the Creator Mind. It is a concept and truth so vast and wondrous which holds the destiny of all within Love and Divine Harmony in such minute complexity as to make the intellect real. And yet, when perceived through the Spirit, through the oneness of your being with Infinite Mind, it becomes knowable, perceivable, and incredibly beautiful in its simplicity.

For, you see, God, Infinite Love, Infinite Mind, Omnipresent Spirit are truly the epitome of simplicity. Love and harmony, and being that which sustains and supports all of Creation is in the wondrous simplicity of being, of "One."

The profundity of this statement must truly be felt through Spirit awareness and not through intellectual hypothesis for that is indeed the dichotomy, the secret of "God's Garden" of inner knowledge. "Except ye be as little children, ye cannot enter the Kingdom of Heaven!" This is a most profound truth stated by the master soul, Jesus, the Christed One. For, you see, the childlike simplicity and childlike purity of thought intention and heart are indeed the very keys that shall unlock the door to your knowing of your God-self Spirit.

Watch the children. Observe them at play and rest. See their innocence, their guilelessness, their utter simplicity of being as the newness of life is experienced in the wonderment of their beings. Look into their eyes and view the trusting nature of open love and laughter as they look out upon the world with eyes filled with acceptance. Truly, the God of All is more seen and felt and touched within the heart of the child than within the great cathedrals, mosques, churches and other structures of rigid religions which are organized control within Humanity's creation.

The oneness of Spirit can indeed only be felt and experienced within the inner senses of self. By practicing meditation, devotion, prayer, affirmations, and focusing the heart and mind inward to where the true reality of God's kingdom reigns, you shall discover the God of your being. And when your inner knowing becomes at one with the Light of Love within your own soul, you shall know the truth of your being, of your Divine part within the cosmos, and you shall know and no longer believe or conceive of that which is nebulous, vague or out of reach. You shall touch the heart of God when you touch the heart of self, for truly, "you are Gods" within your being and are heir to all the wisdom, Love, and abundance which the Father-God Principle has to offer you.

We will talk further of the importance of practices such as meditation and prayer for the unfoldment of consciousness states and the experience of oneness within one's being.

Now, how is mankind, which primarily exists in a reality dedicated to reason, practicality, and limited desires, going to revert back to a childlike vision? How is Humanity, which spends most of its waking and resting hours in the acquisition of wealth, fame, power, and possessions, supposed to attain this spiritual understanding? How shall man come to the realization of his oneness with God within, while desiring and expending time and energy in worldly pursuits? The answer is simple — he won't!

God's grace shall not come to him whose desire and focus is elsewhere. God's loving knowledge flows to those who desire Him, who long for His Light of understanding, who feel the emptiness of the world's vain pursuits and call out to Him in longing reunion of their soul-spirit connection.

Let us look back upon the child as an example. Imagine God is the parent and you are the child. If you are busy playing with your toys and wrapped up with the "fun" of your life, God, the parent, will leave you alone to play. Often, when he calls out to you, your ears are deaf to the call for your focus is upon your play. Yet, when the play becomes tiring and boredom sets in, you long for the Father-Mother's loving arms and attention and you cry out. And when you cry out, God hears.

But he first waits to see if you are truly sure of your desire, if you are truly sure you are tired of your worldly games and are sincere in your longing for His Love and connection. Your parent knows your heart, your mind, your inner desires, and when your cry is given in true longing, in true desire of oneness, your God-self parent comes running to you with outstretched arms, a loving smile, and an overwhelming grace that showers your soul with the Light of Love's reunion and awakening and leaves you overflowing with the nectar of God's Spirit.

If you truly desire your "parent's" knowingness to come upon you, be as the child who puts aside his toys and focuses on the call to his Mother-Father-God Spirit within. Be as the child who gives up the desires of the world and society's demand of success and the hoarding of possessions that eventually possess you. Be as the child who, in loving faith and trust, knows that when he calls out to the Mother-Father-God Principle, it shall come in answer to the cries from the longing in his heart and soul. Be as the child who, in simplicity of soul, opens to receive that which the Parent-God has to give in the fullness of Light and Wisdom. Be as the child who knows no fear but only Love and security within the eternal safety of the Father-Mother's arms. Be as the child whose desire for oneness becomes the goal and finally the realization in truth, the knowing within self of the reality of your God-self, at one with you, now and forever.

Within this period of Earth's history, as stated previously, the energies of transformation and awakening are ever increasing, and the opportunities are greater than ever before upon Terra for the expansion of consciousness and the experience of oneness of Spirit to take place. Many individuals, who at present are locked within worldly thoughts and desires, will feel the gentle nudge of Spirit knocking upon their inner doors of awareness and will feel the pull to a simpler approach to living. They shall hear the distant call of their Spirit-self whispering of a greater, more fulfilling purpose for their lives. They shall sense the futility and the emptiness of their present thoughts and behavior and begin to step away from the mass social consciousness which has them under rigid control. They shall seek out a new and more purposeful existence which coincides with their inner call to great harmony, freedom, and spiritual awareness.

From those whose righteous behavior and judgmental thoughts separate them from themselves in false superior perception to those who seemingly are lost in evil doing and wrongness of actions, beware! For even the most seeming of evil action and person have the Spirit of God within their being. He who judges and condemns his brother in conscious judgment condemns himself. He judges himself by his own lack of perception and universal acceptance of the Brotherhood of All Consciousness. Allow your brother to be, to act, to follow and choose the way, the path closest to his own heart and desires, and judge his choices not! Be within the choosing of your path in loving acceptance and awareness of your responsibility to your being.

For, truly, upon all levels of existence and development, "You are responsible for your own evolution and soul expansion, now and always, and your brother is responsible for his." Pity not those who, through your perception, seem to have lost their way, but love them because the God-self within is leading them in its own knowing way and will bring to them the message of Spirit when they are ready and willing to hear.

Give freely of your words and thoughts of encouragement and Love, yet be not a part of their energy unless it is uplifting and harmonious to your own because your own expansion must be allowed freedom of expression. If you take upon your being the responsibility of another's energy and evolution, you are asking for pain and setbacks in your own growth. Allow others to be in the fullness of their freedom of choice. Allow others to be who they are in loving acceptance, and you shall see the transformation of your being into God-self awareness for is not the God of all life totally accepting of all? Is not the Infinite Mind fully and completely in allowance of all Creation and its free expression in all ways? Is not your Father-Mother-God Principle in unconditional non-judgment of all life forms upon all dimensions? Is not the Lord of your being ever loving to you and all creatures now and always, ever patient, ever understanding?

Yes, of course, because, you see, the Lord of your being is the Lord of All and being part and parcel of All His Creation, He could not, would not now or ever judge, condemn, or cause hurt to Himself for He is All. All that is is all that is!

When one, through criticism and judgment, sets himself up as judge and jury with regard to another's behavior or actions, he becomes imprisoned within his own limitation of concepts of good and bad, right and wrong, and therefore condemns himself through self-superior, ego righteousness to the fate of the darkness of limited perception. Beware of spiritual fervor and righteous concepts. Your own place and part within the structure of God's universal Laws of Harmony and Love are the same and equal to your brother's, no matter the level of your brother's state of evolution. Your own perceptive capability is unable to determine the level or evolutionary place within or upon your brother, so cease in this useless pursuit for it serves you not. Instead, seek your own freedom through the gift of freedom to all others to be what they will. Liberate yourself through Love and acceptance of self and all life forms at all levels.

The oneness of Spirit is the oneness of all life forms, and the complete and total allowance of all universal Creation to evolve within its own rate through loving acceptance. When Jesus spoke the universal truth to "love your neighbor as yourself," he restated the Law of Oneness, the Law of Divine Principle that we and all life are one Spirit, one essence, equal in the eyes of He who fashioned the stars; and that through the expression, understanding, and practice of the vibration of Love of all things great and small, we would be practicing the purpose, presence, and power of the God-Force Principle in operation and design. Through this act we become one with the Spirit within ourselves and within all of Creation. To become "one with" means to align yourself in likeness of purpose in Spirit and in destiny. This is the Law of Divine Harmony as well as the reality of the Truth Principle.

Become one within you, oh Humanity. Practice the loving acceptance and presence of your God-self and all God-selves within all life. Perceive your own truth, your own path, and allow all others the same freedom.

"May peace and harmony reign on Earth!"

III

♦

"Thou Art the Truth"

♦

The struggle of Humanity to pursue truth and justice in the outer world of form has undoubtedly resulted in the formation and structure of a society "gone mad," with complexity and confusion reigning over the throne of instability and empty promise. Within man's inner being reigns the true King of Knowledge, Justice, and Truth, but he sees it not for the credence and validity of inner perception and self-trust is virtually unknown in modern society. Yet it is this very inner trust that shall lead man home from the turmoil and heartache which the world of form and senses has offered and supplied with disastrous results.

As Humanity becomes tired and bored with the fruits of earthly delights and begins to realize it wants and longs for something greater, something intangible to the senses, it shall ultimately turn within to discover its own truth. Through that realization begins a new world order based upon individual and collective understanding. Each consciousness, each life form is and always has been its own truth.

"Ye are the truth."

As this statement is expressed, your intellect is immediately poised in the position of doubt, self-denial, and disbelief; and yet, this is the "Law of Divine Dispensation" that all consciousness carries within it its own truth at all levels. This Divine law is complete in its formulations and expression for it incorporates in its entirety all of Creation, all of dimensional experience and understanding.

Infinite Mind, being all to all within and without all, gives complete allowance and freedom to all so each one can be his own truth in consciousness expressed.

As your eyes look out upon your world and perceive in limitation through your senses of perception, your conceptual understanding is used to the idea that within this great and wondrous universe there must be a "Great Truth" to be found "out there," and that once found, it shall prove to make sense out of the madness and confusion that is upon this world. Yet, I say unto you that there is no Great Truth to be discovered outside of your own being, for all truth is your own and to be known within yourself. You, the real you, the God-self, the eternal and infinite self, is the one and only truth.

Again, we return to One. It is so simple yet so confusing to the intellect. That, my friends, is the treasure, the secret stored within the safekeeping of your inner being and the one place mankind has failed to look.

Within the play of man's greed, we find the analogy of coveted treasures of gold and precious gems safely buried in a secret place, never to be discovered except by the use of the "secret maps" which identify the location of the buried treasures. He who is lucky enough to obtain a copy of the secret map is the one who shall discover and claim the great treasure and become rich from the bounty.

It is the same within each individual consciousness. Buried deep within yourself is the treasure of God-spirit, alive and well, eternal and all-knowing. You are in need of the secret map that shows the location and method of discovery (such as is found in this book and others which point the way). Master guides and teachers proclaim that "heaven is within thee." There are techniques for self-discovery, meditation, prayer, affirmations, visualization; and, finally, there is the practice of diving deep within oneself to discover the Pearls of Wisdom, the Kingdom of Heaven, the Treasure of Treasures, which, when once found and tasted, shall give you riches untold: Wisdom, Love, Joy, Fulfillment, and Truth; Truth that "Thou art That," "Thou art the Truth," your God-self manifest as man within form.

Yet no book, no guide, no religious sect or philosophy can give you that which is your own in Divine ownership. That desire and will of your real self, that unquenching thirst for Divine awareness, is the only call that will be heard and answered by Spirit. All else are but guides and helping hands to your experience of God-Consciousness.

No amount of intellectual reasoning, no greatly heralded university degrees, no amount of worldly knowledge will add to the wisdom of your God-self, now or ever, nor shall these things bring you the moment of grace when your being is showered with the knowingness of Spirit. Only your childlike purity of desire to be one with the Father shall lead you to His door within your heart. "Knock and the door shall be opened unto you; ask and you shall receive," is the Divine Law of God's Will that all life be guaranteed when that which you seek in Spirit understanding comes from purity in thought and intention and with a longing in your soul for the truth within you.

God-Infinite-Father Principle desires all Creation to receive that which it desires through the use of Infinite Mind power. All are capable of manifesting all wants and needs if they are in understanding of how the laws of manifestation work and their proper application. As long as your belief within self is aligned with God's Infinite Mind power, "all things are possible." If you truly believe, then you shall receive that for which you ask. You shall surely receive.

It is the proper use of focused thought, desire, and the knowing within self that that which you have asked for is already given to you, is already yours now. Doubt and disbelief are the enemies of your true self for they thwart all good desires and prevent you from receiving that which is your spiritual birthright as heir to the Kingdom of God within. Doubt and disbelief are simply giving power to the darkness of separation between your soul and Spirit, between that which you truly are and that which you in limitation perceive yourself to be. When doubt raises its head and your eyes see it for its true motive, it is but fear. It is the fear of knowing the power of which the true self is really capable, and the responsibility of that power. When we doubt, we set up walls about us, closing off the magic of inner understanding and expanded aware-ness. What we are saying is, "because I cannot see it, because it is not part of my present reality and perception, I do not believe in its reality or truth," thereby closing the door to the entering of Spirit.

The child does not disbelieve or doubt. All that is told to him he believes totally. Santa Claus, the Easter Bunny, and many other stories which the child hears he believes within his trust. So why is it so difficult for the responsible adult to trust and believe, even though his outer senses do not validate that which he inwardly feels? Why does the mature mind of reason limit itself from experiencing the magical wonderment within? Is it because of the pressures of social conscious-ness, the need for conformity, and the acceptance of the concept of right and wrong, possible and impossible, within the framework of man's present view of himself and the world about him?

One hundred years ago, the acceptance by the mass social conscious-ness of the possible and impossible made it impossible for a man to walk on the moon or for a jet plane to fly from continent to continent within a matter of hours. This was a totally accepted impossibility. It was simply beyond the scope of man's ability. Yet, two thousand years ago, a single man who, being one in consciousness with his God-Father-self, was easily able to fly, walk upon water, raise the dead, heal the sick, manifest food and wine, and more. Yet, these deeds even today are viewed by a majority of Humanity to be impossible and out of reach or context with daily, normal existence; or, if they did happen at all, it was through a fluke, a mistake, or possibly because God chose Jesus, the magician, to stand out among men to show them his "tricks" in order to fool them into believing in the impossible.

Yet, Jesus, the Christed One, did indeed perform these feats for mankind to reveal to them the possibilities within them, when and if they could believe and trust in the God-Father Principle within. That truly magnificent master teacher placed his being among the throngs, not to be worshipped but to act as an example for all to see and follow — that man united with God could accomplish anything he willed or desired, as long as he was aligned in like purpose with the Greater Will and Power of Infinite Love and Mind. When Jesus spoke the words, "All that I have done, ye can also do, and greater works shall ye do in my name," this master soul was so totally aligned with his Father-God-self that he no longer viewed his personal ego self for it had become one with the ocean of God's Spirit within him. Those words were not meant to convey that in the name of Jesus were the acts to be performed, but in the name of the Holy Spirit, God-Father Principle, the greater self within. He clearly stated that all the works he did, all could do, and even greater feats than he had displayed, using the power of the Divine Law of manifestation, the Infinite God-Mind energy and knowledge therein.

If you were to ask a modern-day, God-fearing Christian if indeed he believed it possible to enact and perform the raising of the dead or to walk upon water, he would most likely say that it was impossible for the normal person to do so, or that only Jesus, who was the only Son of God, or God, Himself, could indeed do these acts. And he would be partially correct. For, yes, the normal man who is unaware of his God-self connection and who lives within the limited perception of man's belief could not do that which Jesus did.

And yet, if a normal man were to expand his limited perception of himself and align his energy and soul with the God-Force Principle through cosmic awakening, he indeed would be able to call upon the forces of Power-Light-Spirit within and do all that Jesus, the Christed One, was able to do, and more. That is truly what is in store for the new man of God-Mind awakening at this time. That is the picture of the future within this dimension as it expands into fourth-dimensional frequency. That is the destiny of all who align themselves with the God-Force Principle and truthfully are able to say, "I and my Father are One."

And when the future child looks to its parent and inquisitively asks, "Mother, what is truth?" the parent of tomorrow will lovingly take the child into its arms and say, "You are the truth, my child, you are the truth!" So be it.

Oh, Infinite Father, may all men, through your grace and loving Spirit, come to the realization of their oneness with Thee and truly discover their truth within, the Eternal Truth of their Spirit "I Am" self.

Om. Peace. Bliss. Understanding!

IV

*The God-Force
Principle and the
Ascension of Man*

✦

Within the timelessness and formlessness of the All That Is, we of the dimensions of higher frequency prefer to term this Infinite Mind the "God-Force Principle" for it denotes the many various and unlimited aspects of which we all are a part and expresses the Father Spirit, which is all-encompassing. Spirit, the Source, Infinite Mind – all are virtually the same description of Allness of Being which is omnipresent within all, and surrounds all. The dream of Creation and third-dimensional existence, and the accepted and agreed-upon dramas of complexity and singleness of God's purpose within all structures of His Being are truly beyond description and evaluation through the intellectual approach. The experience of God's Presence is the only true way of knowing that which is beyond preconception.

The God-Force Principle, which is your home, your self and all else that you perceive in the world of form as well as in those dimensions of infinite number which are presently beyond your knowing, are one and related to each other. They are one through "Infinite-Mind Stuff" and penetrate all Creation within the God-Force Principle thought. In truth, there is no separation within this principle, just as within your physical body, those areas which are in illness or disease affect all other organs and aspects of the physical structure in their connection. In order for the physical body to express wholeness (oneness), all aspects must be correctly functioning and in harmonious agreement. Within all levels of being, from the microcosmic to the macrocosmic proportions of Light intensity and formless dimensional experience, it is the same, the interwoven link of all thought Creation.

That is precisely how and why that of my thought and being is able to communicate with and through you now. You must understand that your thought and God's thought are not separate or unique because the oneness of being is apparent, obvious and open to my being even as it is to yours when you are operating in the higher-self connection and non-physical dimensions. The operation and attunement of my being and thought with yours is truly not as complex as you might imagine for it takes place within the timelessness and infinite aspects of you. I am in oneness with you and in oneness with All That Is.

When certain principles of consciousness and formless thought are more readily accepted and understood by you, you shall experience even greater levels of our communication process within. The more subtle forms of experience and perception shall be made available to you in greater degree.

Now, the wondrous God-Force Principle that you are, and that I am, and that All is, operates within and about all Creation and thought-form projections. Within each experience of its formless identity and principles, it connects, communes, and is in Love with All That Is of Itself. And All That Is of Itself is All That Is.

Nothing exists outside of the God-Force Principle. Nothing! All is within the heart and within the Love-sustaining principles of thought which make up the God-Force Principle. The love that is within your experience of physical embodiment is, at its highest, but a taste, a mere fragment of the all-encompassing, unconditional, non-judgmental, all-understanding, all-wise Love presence of your own God-self, linked and connected with the God-Force Principle! Love on this infinite scale could not be compared to anything in your earthly relationships or physical identification for, in its infinite aspects, it transcends all separation, all conditions, all individual experience. It shines its sweet radiance from within the infinite loving heart of the Father outward to all, and then inward, back upon itself in everlasting waves of blissful, oceanic embraces quite beyond anything imaginable even to the most evolved and advanced beings of formless Light.

The angelic kingdoms, in their greatness of being and Light vibration, the gods of celestial Light and hierarchy of universal harmony lower their Divine eyes and humble themselves to this almighty, all-loving simplicity which is the God-Force Principle in expression through them and through all. The infinite power of this force termed Love is truly beyond knowingness and can be experienced in evolving scales of receptivity and allowance as each entity comes unto itself in humility and understanding of its own true nature and connection with the Love that it is.

You and all consciousness, all life-forms within all dimensions of being, are created and living within this ever evolving, ever loving, all-knowing Principle. All are swimming in the limitless ocean of Spirit and, through your dimension of form and seeming matter, would infer the individualization and separation of consciousness. In fact, this is not so. All beings are one in a greater sense as they move, en masse, within layers and sublayers of conscious Spirit-blending. Although they are in a relatively unconscious perception of third-dimensional vibration, they perceive themselves limited to that particular form within which they reside.

As the God-Force Principle exceeds frequencies of Light energy, descending and blending with your own energies and those of mankind, you will experience, even as you are experiencing now, the quickening and ascension of your perceptual field, thereby allowing access to higher vibratory dimensions. All are moving forward and upward into this field of perception. As the vibrations of Spirit and form become less dense, you will experience sensory levels far beyond that which have limited you to your seeming reality. The five normal senses which you have relied upon for your Earth experience shall also undergo a heightened perceptual awareness, thereby allowing the eyes to see greater fields of color, the ears to sense inner vibratory Creation, and so on. These five senses shall still be used by the new man of heightened awareness, and yet, their sole reliance on fields of information and perception shall be less important and looked upon as mere tools to be used while in form. They shall be seen for what they are.

As man opens his awareness of newly found freedom, he shall be responsible for that information received, and for the utilization of expansion within his being. Inwardly, all beings who desire the quickening of God-self innately choose to expedite these energies in a positive way, thereby enhancing their own evolutionary levels.

Mankind has yet to awaken to the infinite possibilities which lie within him. When they are activated, he shall create new and unparalleled vistas of creative opportunity and advancement upon Terra. This is what awaits all who choose the Light and desire greater awareness. Those who do not choose, because of their ignorance of those heightened vibrations, shall suffer the fate of the cellular breakdown of their bodies and minds as the greatly increased energies intensify. All of Creation is in the process of great expansion and vibratory enhancement. That is why our work is of such importance at this time, because time as you know it is indeed running out.

With reference to the intensifying vibrations and energies of Light which are flooding all of material and nonmaterial Creation, we spoke previously about the cellular breakdown of bodies and minds of those who choose not to walk the Path of Light. This was not meant to judge or condemn or to place fear within your heart. Those who would inwardly choose that downward cycle shall not perish as there is truly no death; yet they shall not be allowed to continue within the finer structure of the impending higher frequencies. They shall be transferred to another quadrant of the galaxy to continue evolving at their own pace.

All beings are in the process of choosing their camps at this time and are creating that reality for themselves, either through Love or fear. Those who choose either way truly have nothing to fear for the survival of their soul is guaranteed, whether in form or not. The advantage of choosing Light or expansion is unparalleled at this point in your history of incarnate existence. At this time you and all of mankind will be witness to the Divine Hand of God reaching out from within all Creation. This is a most momentous and exciting era in which to be in form upon this plane because you shall witness events and experiences which will transform Terra into a paradise of heavenly proportion. Once the Earth Mother has completed her birthing process and succeeded in burning off the dross accumulated over eons of human willfulness and thoughtlessness, she will settle into her newly found responsibility, working hand-in-hand with the new man, the new caretaker of this planet. As an evolving, aware being of immense compassion and patience, she will take her place among the enlightened stars as a cosmic way station for all extraterrestrial and interdimensional life support, and she will enjoy the higher vibration of loving proportions as she stands complete in health as a part of the unified, collective, enlightened confederation of planets in this solar system. Praise be to that momentous occasion which is waiting to unfold in all its Divine glory. The destructive energies are truly cleansing energies, and mankind will ultimately become aware of this. When the purification is complete, mankind shall know and understand that the awakening and birthing process is intended to create anew that which has been depleted and destroyed through ignorance and folly.

V

♦

The Awakening of
Terra and the
Second Advent of
Christ

♦

And then upon the multitude there shone a great and brilliant
Light, a Light of a thousand suns, and the people, in fear, fell to
their knees upon the ground. And then, from within, a voice was heard
by all to say:

"Behold, I cometh to walk amongst you to share in thy consciousness all that I Am and to reveal the Light of my being unto thee and to
remove thy sorrows and fears. Awaken, my children of form, for thy
dream is finished and it is time to know thyself and to know thy God.
Awaken! Awaken! For I am come unto thee now to show the way, the
truth, and the Light. Awaken, my children, for I am thee and thou art I.
Awaken! Awaken!

"And the darkness of their minds and the fear within their hearts
disappeared as the day of the Lord was upon them. And all understood
and all opened their eyes for the first time and saw the world anew: a
world of Light, laughter and abundance; a world filled with the Love of
Divine acceptance and peace. The past was forgotten as if the entire
history of Humanity had been but a dream. Man no longer made war
upon his brothers, and sickness and death became no more than a
distant memory."

In the days of my last and final incarnation upon Terra, life was much more simple in many ways, and I enjoyed the quiet, monastic approach which allowed me a great amount of time for contemplation and dedication to God-thought and the teachings of our Lord, Jesus Christ. Part of those teachings included the belief that soon the world would again be visited and finally redeemed through the Second Coming of Jesus, the Christ.

Within the context of Christian doctrine, we all assumed that Jesus himself, accompanied by his angelic host and guardianship, would be returning in flames of glory, with trumpets sounding and angels singing. This was the belief and faith in the Biblical doctrine set down by the Christian fathers. It was, indeed, quite strict and precisely followed to the word and letter written. This was the way of the faith and trust of the simple, monastic brothers, even though it was suppressed and limited. Yet, many could see past the written word and view the greater, deeper teaching and symbolism within. Because of the strictness of thought, they kept the understanding to themselves for the most part, not wanting to place themselves in awkward positions with the senior fathers of the Church. Within that era, however, there was still much "magic" within the confines of Church theology, and many secret, mystical teachings were shared behind guarded doors.

The very concept of faith within the Church regarding Jesus' abilities to perform magical feats and mystical miracles beyond man's normal existence was fully accepted as being part and parcel of the power of his God union. Yet, within the structure of the Church, these abilities were limited to Jesus' kinship with the Father and viewed as his and his alone, for he was considered as the only Son of God, and only he carried within him this power.

The rigid belief structure of the Church did not approve of man's having free thinking or being personally able to attain God's vision. That would have decreased the power and hold of the Church over the flock. Control and conformity were, as they still are, the doctrine which is enforced within the Church. All acts or behavior which went outside of that organized thought system were dissuaded and looked down upon. However, at times when certain individuals within the Church's fold were viewed as performing miracles and feats of sainthood, the elder fathers were forced to concede their strict line and proclaim the mystical powers and saintliness of these individuals, often after their death.

Unfortunately, many people were put to death by the Church itself because of its rigid position, and only after the death of the awakened saint did the Church proclaim their canonization into sainthood.

It has always been thus when man attempts to control and enslave his fellow man through fear or belief in a fearful God of judgment and vengeance. I am saddened to say also that there have been more wars, more hatred, and more pain inflicted within the teachings of Christianity than within any other faith. Sadly enough, the dichotomy is that within the gentle, loving Spirit of our master, Jesus, and his ways and teachings, he always proclaimed Love, not revenge or forced control over the beliefs or paths of others. To turn the other cheek when smitten was a thought system directly opposite the Old Testament's proclamation, "Vengeance is mine, sayeth the Lord" or "An eye for an eye, a tooth for a tooth."

So we view the confusion within the concepts and teachings, and yet the Church continues this confusion by asking its flock not to question but to obey all commands, all tenets, and all commandments within both the Old and New Testament doctrines.

Within my monastic life, I was inwardly guided to follow my own contemplative understanding, and because of this, I usually kept my experiences, thoughts and visions to myself. The doctrine was there, and I followed it to the letter outwardly while inwardly, I listened to my own higher truth. Yet when I had my first experience of cosmic awakening, all belief and concept of Church doctrine disappeared in the Light of my own God-knowingness. It was then that I truly understood the truth beyond and behind the teachings of my Lord Jesus and his oneness with the Father-God Principle.

It was then that I understood the true purpose and proclamation of his second coming. Within my being I saw and understood that man was on the threshold of a new birth, a new awakening of his Christ-self or God-self and that indeed that was the meaning of his second and final advent into Earth and man's consciousness.

Now, in this era, as I move through various realities of dimensional experience with my brothers in our work, we add our energy to the dawning of this Christ Consciousness; and I perceive the future of that initial vision and understanding and see it transpiring just as envisioned. I see the vast Light frequencies flowing within and upon all dimensional experiences on all planes. I feel the quickening within man's consciousness coming alive, stirring in its sleep yet faintly hearing the call of Spirit's whisper within. I see the changes upon Terra as she, the vibrant living being, awakens to her place and responsibility in this sector of the galaxy. I see the awesome energies of change and renewal bubble up within her planetary body and the impending destruction of much of Humanity upon her. I see the fear and terror and the subsequent peace and harmony as her health and energy are restored through the awakening and transformation of her being and man's consciousness.

Much is upon you now, oh Humanity, and much is yet to come into your experience. Your awakening is at hand. Your birth is at hand. The God of Light within beckons you to now fling open the gates of consciousness and welcome His presence within you to restore harmony, balance, and peace within your being and upon Terra before it is too late. Will you hear the call? Will you cast away your old concepts and invite in the new, true plan of your own destiny? Or will your deaf ears continue in deafness and ignorance of your true state and place within the cosmic order? The choice is always your own as your free will is your gift, but the moment of choice is upon you now, and the gates of heaven are about to swing open, whether or not you are prepared. The awakening of Terra is here now, and the energies of opportunity are great as all the Forces of Light are unified and ready to aid you in your knowing and unfoldment. What are your priorities, oh man, that before you stands the gatekeeper of God's Kingdom, yet you see him not? Open your eyes and ears to all that is about you. See you not the signs of change? See you not that the day of the Lord is here now, today?

The second advent of Christ shall not come with loud trumpets and chariots of fire but shall come quietly, gently, to your open consciousness, and it shall flood you with the pure knowing of God's Love and presence within you. The return of the Christ is the rebirth of man's inner understanding through awakened Light and cosmic union with his own personal God-self. United as one, the Christed Man of God shall bring in the dawn of the new Golden Age that awaits in peace, harmony, and the Divine understanding that all is one Spirit and all are equal. The Christ-Consciousness fully awakened within man shall, indeed, through the power and will of the Father-God Principle, transform the energies of this plane into a paradise heretofore unknown and unheard of, and you shall walk and talk hand in hand with the God of your being. The veils which separate the frequency of vibration between the third-dimensional experience and the fourth- and fifth-dimensional vibrations shall be rent asunder, and the freedom of movement and expression therein shall be shared and understood. Form and formlessness shall be perceived, and in close communion, Spirit shall be seen and felt by all.

Those entities who are not in physical form shall be easily heard and understood, and communication shall be simplified since thought shall be instantly known. Honesty and truth shall be the norm since any dishonest intention shall be perceived by all. You shall indeed communicate with all life forms because the blending of Spirit energies shall bring forth your knowingness with all of God's creatures. Love shall be freely expressed by all, to all, as the Light of understanding shines brightly through each soul-spirit union. This is your destiny, oh, God-man; this is your future.

You are God! Is it not a wonderment upon your intellect to outwardly make this statement? Does it not resonate deeply within your soul as the words are spoken? Somewhere within your consciousness the knowingness of your "I Am" Spirit resides and now calls to you for awakening and remembrance of your true nature. Somewhere deep within, you are growing tired of your dream within form and are longing for a greater Love, a greater truth, a more fulfilling life complete with trust, hope, and expanded awareness. Are you not growing weary of continual incarnation into form and the subsequent dreams of the scenes within your play, with all the various roles you have performed and still play?

Would you not like to know your true nature and experience the joy of your open freedom, being the observer instead of the actor caught up in believing his role is the reality of life instead of the temporary performance upon the stage of Earth? For, indeed, your role upon form is truly temporary and your future is uncertain, for the angel-of-death transition could take you at any given moment from your acting part in Earth's play. No one is sure or secure within form for there are so many dangers that present themselves to disrupt and destroy the physical body. The uncertainty of physical existence was meant to convey to the mind of man the significance of establishing the God-self connection so that, in Spirit, he could override fear and disruption through the power of his God-Force oneness in conscious awareness.

To the God-man, nothing is impossible. There is no feat too great, no challenge too difficult. The Christ Consciousness within man, once united with man's consciousness, can veritably move mountains, part oceans, proclaim to the winds to cease, and they will indeed cease.

Oh man, you are God, and yet know it not. Cease identifying with the limitations of your physical body for you are Divine Spirit focused within the physical. When you see and feel your God-self within, you shall surely know and proclaim, "I Am that I Am!"

Your body is your temple where you shall meet your God. Your body is your vehicle used to gain experience and growth upon the physical plane. Your body is a wondrous machine that, when properly taken care of through right thought and fresh food and water consumption, can serve you well. Your body, however, is not your self. Your self is a Divine spark of the Infinite God-mind, and once known, it may truly refine and transform the body in subcellular fashion so as to make it deathless, beyond disease.

Your doubt arises and says, "impossible," and yet, again, there is the example of the ability of the Master Jesus to ascend the death of the physical state, reassemble the atoms and cellular formation of the body through God-Force Mind, and through that Creation of the omnidimensional body, attain the freedom of movement between dimensional vibrations. Jesus' ascension and knowledge of the God-Force connection was complete and total. The creation and use of the formation of the omnidimensional body was but another capability of his oneness with his Father-God Principle in totality of awareness.

Your reality is your truth, and your reality is limited to your thoughts and perceptions of yourself and this world. Expand the thought and you shall expand your possibilities. Expand your possibilities and you shall expand your own self-awareness. Expand your self-awareness and you shall find the God-self within.

Oh man, tear down your walls of limitation of thought and self-doubt and see yourself as you truly are: unlimited Light, unlimited Spirit, forever beingness. Awaken to your Christ-self consciousness now, this moment, this day! "Be still and know that I am God."

Within the stillness of your being rests the eternal cause-spirit, and you shall know your "I Am" through the doorway of meditation. Through your quiet mind, void of thought, comes the Light of God to your conscious awareness. When the cup becomes empty, the Infinite Spirit fills you to overflowing with the knowingness of the I Am consciousness. Upon realization of your oneness with Spirit, the Father-God Principle takes place and you experience liberation. The enlightenment of your being in oneness is your only reason for being upon physical form at this time. If it were that your eyes were opened and the realization was upon you, the need for further incarnations would cease to be because you would be free.

This schoolroom of Terra has been ever patient with you in your learning and in your fellow men's perpetration of destructive greed upon the oceans, forests, atmosphere and land, but now her patience is at an end. You shall bear witness to great and awesome energies of change upon her body, and within that change, you shall find a new Earth being born. It is, therefore, imperative to connect with the higher vibrations of Spirit and Light within if you are to become part of the new order of God's Kingdom on Terra.

This wondrous living being, Terra, is also awakening to a higher state of consciousness with the advent and influx of Light energies. Soon she shall be born to awareness of herself and her place within the galactic order of planetary beings within the solar system. She will take her place among the heavenly stars within the cosmos, fully aware of her responsibility to herself and all life which is within and upon her beauteous body. She shall awaken to her purpose, task, and destiny within God's firmament. The new energies stir within her even now as

I speak. Do you not feel her beneath your feet, moving within a dawning of the new day of her reckoning and grace? Do you not see the signs all about you of her readiness to implement the renewal of her depletion due to man's thoughtless acts upon her being?

Within yourself you know the truth of these words and feel that change in process. Attune yourself to your own inner sensitivity with the Earth Mother and her energies. Align with the forces of the elements about you and make them your ally in these coming days, for surely the elements shall revolt and winds and storms shall gather in force of such intensity that your buildings shall not stand against them. The waters of the Mother shall rise against you in fury and abandon. Cling to your God-self, not out of fear but out of Love. Trust that all is moving and working toward a greater good.

As the dawn of Terra's awakening comes into fullness, no part of your planet shall be spared disruption, yet certain areas shall be safer than others for the sustenance of life and necessary elements therein. Follow your inner guidance to these havens of higher ground and strong foundation. Go to where your God-spirit tells you for the land shall seem to be in defiance of all natural order and past climatic patterns. Where it was warm and dry, it shall become cold and wet, and vice versa. You should be able to move freely as Spirit guides you to your own safe place. What was safe today may not be safe tomorrow, so always let the inner knowing be your trusted guide and ally. Make the connection now through stillness of thought, and practice meditation to increase your oneness with Spirit so you may know and understand that which is upon you in the forces of nature, wherever you may be. When those inner feelings come upon you, listen well and act for it is your spirit-self warning you and sensing that which is to come.

I have witnessed that which shall come to pass. I have seen the terror-filled eyes, the fear within man's heart as the Earth abandons all her elements, unleashing destruction upon Humanity and all life there-in, in her attempt to regain her balance and well-being. I have seen the coming floods, earthquakes, famine, and massive destruction which await in the near future as Terra shakes off the dross of lower vibration and the negativity of the dense thought-forms planted through eons of man's history upon her. I have seen the faces of continents shift and alter within a single day's time as her oceans replace coastal areas, states, and countries. I have seen the sinking of land masses and the rising of others as the entire shifting of submerged areas causes them to re-emerge from the ocean's depths. I have seen the time of sorrows as many relinquish their physical bodies through fear, hardship, and the loss of all possessions and faith in themselves and in the God within.

These things are upon you now, oh Humanity. Heed the signs of change and act, not out of fear but out of your own God-spirit. As your fellow men fall in fear and loss, be strong and faithful in your resolve and determination to carry forth through the God-power within you. Choose the good, the higher road of your Light beingness, and through your inner guidance, your feet shall be directed wisely.

Fear not, for all is in God's hands, and His Love and Light are within and about you always.

Oh, loving Father-God within, awaken thy children to their God-self and to their awareness of you as themselves. Open the gates of thy Light and let the darkness of men's minds be swept away in thy Love forever. Amen.

VI

♦

Going Within

♦

So far, within this teaching, you have heard us speak often of your true God-self within and the necessity of meeting your God and truth through the gate of your inner self. It is important that we make clear to you the importance of understanding that all wisdom, Light and truth are indeed within you, and that you are responsible for the inner journey of discovery. No one can take you home but yourself, and your God awaits you now for your return.

Going within simply means taking your conscious awareness of outer reality and turning it upon itself, or focusing from without upon that inner reality. It is a process and practice that is essential in your own growth and self-understanding. It is both a science and an art which truly must be mastered if you will know yourself in fullness of being.

Your present perception of yourself is and has been limited to those thoughts, feelings, and beliefs which were given to you by your parents and past programming, either in past-life patterns or present-day childhood rearing. All that you have come to understand of yourself has been through experiences and beliefs.

You look upon your body, face, and form and see a man or a woman endowed with certain features, talents and abilities. You identify quite clearly and astutely with your role and character. This dream of reality

created is, however, not reality but an illusion. It is a
have created for yourself in order to learn certain lessons
ice growth in areas and issues for your final act of coming
to exactly where you are now and to your own awakening and self-discovery.

As I say these words, repeat after me, within your mind, until you
feel the vibration of truth resounding within you:

I am not my body!
I am not my mind!
I am not my thoughts!
I am not my fears!
I am not my talents and abilities!

After you have repeated these thoughts within and have felt their
power, follow the same process again, using the affirmations of truth of
that which you truly are:

I am Light – I AM!
I am Love – I AM!
I am God-Spirit Principle – I AM!
I am beyond form – I AM!
I am beyond birth and death – I AM!
I am Infinite Love – I AM!
I AM!! God!! I AM!!

This simple exercise is meant to redirect your focus of perceptual
beliefs from illusion to reality, from the false to the real. As the exercise
of repeating these expanded thoughts over and over within your mind is
done, the subconscious programming patterns of belief, perception, and
limitation begin to slowly crumble and lose their power over you, for
truth is stronger than untruth, and Light is stronger than darkness.
Within your inner knowing, you know the truth of the thoughts therein
as your soul reaches upward toward union with your Spirit God-self. For,
in reality, you are truly formless essence, temporarily encased at this

time within a physical body. And although you are performing your part within your dream, your focus of perception does not have to be locked up and limited to the physical drama. You can go within and move beyond your present limitation of perception and view your true nature as God-self Principle. It is a matter of refocusing and redirecting your thoughts, beliefs and behavior to your inner reality and your inner Light through practice, technique, and will. Your desire for Light shall be your guide to the Inner Kingdom. Your longing for peace, Love and union with your God shall be your path to liberation and spiritual understanding.

Going within encompasses prayer, meditation, inner contemplation, focused affirmations, visualization, and mantra, using all methods, all practices for inner expansion. Chose one or two or all that you shall use and begin with that which feels good or right for you. All are merely methods to realign yourself with Spirit and higher frequencies of vibration so that your connection will be forthcoming. Do not be too attached to your techniques or methods for all are equal tools to be used to gain the prize. Once the prize is attained, you shall no longer need the tools, but for now they are your ladder to the heights of yourself, so use them.

Of all these methods to be used in your spiritual search, we would suggest that the most important is meditation. Through meditation and the act of diving deep into the ocean of yourself, the prize shall be found most quickly. As we previously stated, all methods are good and should be used if they flow with your need, yet meditation is the one tool that shall surely lead you directly home if it is pursued and practiced with diligence and devotion.

Your God-self rests patiently within you, and it is there where you shall discover it. The act and process of meditation shall guide you to your Divine inheritance and kingdom. This is the true substantive definition of "going within," and there are many techniques widely used in this "science of soul knowledge." We would like to give you a simple method and one that shall help you begin your process.

First, let us begin with a brief discussion of the importance of breath and consciousness states. Within all life forms upon Terra, breathing is a part of life's process and within man it becomes a yardstick and measurement of man's emotional, psychological, and spiritual states. All things work as one within the physical system and all are related. In other words, physical, mental, and emotional states are interrelated and converge within the system of man. For example, if one is emotionally or psychologically ill at ease, his rapid breathing reveals his state and is viewed perceptively by it. When one is calm and at peace with life and himself, his breathing will be perceived as slow, rhythmic, and in alignment with his state of balance.

When approaching a setting of meditation, one should first begin with several cleansing breaths: (1) breathe deeply, (2) fill the lungs, (3) hold the breath for 10 to 20 seconds, (4) expel through the mouth with force, and (5) repeat the process.

After this process, begin focusing on slower, longer, more rhythmic breaths. Breathe in through the nostrils slowly, fill the lungs, hold for 20 seconds, or for that length of time which feels comfortable, then exhale slowly through the nostrils until the breath is completely expelled. Sit in stillness within the out breath, then repeat the process.

Now, we begin!

Sit comfortably with your back straight, hands on your lap or resting comfortably on your knees. It is all right if you would rather lie down with your back straight. The advantage to sitting is that it allows the mind to stay alert and aware. Often, when one is lying down, the physical system, as well as the subconscious, which is programmed through sleep patterns, has a tendency to drift off to a lesser state of wakefulness.

Now, sitting comfortably, begin your cleansing breaths. Ten should be sufficient at the beginning. After completing the cleansing breaths, begin the slower, rhythmic breaths.

Eyes should be closed and focused upward, placing a light tension upon the third eye chakra center at the point between the eyebrows. A gentle, upward glance is sufficient to bring energies to focus in this area which is directly linked through "nadis," or etheric nerve centers within the physical body, to the pineal gland center at the back of the head.

As you sit with your eyes closed and focused, being alert and aware of your breath and the slow, rhythmic patterns, stay focused on your breath. Your mind will wander from thought to thought, which is natural. Do not attempt to restrain it for it shall rebel and your peace shall be lost. Instead, allow your mind to do what it wants, while keeping your focus upon slowing the breath even more. Physiologically, as the breath becomes slower and gentler, your mind and thoughts shall begin to slow down as well. As your breath slows down, begin to focus on the mind as the observer of your thoughts, without becoming involved or identifying with them. As your thoughts become yet slower, and as your awareness is able to retain its focus as "the observer" without becoming attached to each thought, you shall witness a most amazing thing. Your mind shall gain more and more peace, and your inner self shall come closer and closer to your inner sight and perception therein.

Do not be in awe or surprised if within yourself you experience energy surges, visions, lights, or flashes of scenes that have passed before or are yet to come. All of these are but preliminary signposts of the higher vibrational frequencies being activated within your psychic center (pineal gland) and the awakening of your inner sight. "If thine eye be single, thy whole body shall be filled with Light." This is but the forerunner of greater awakenings to come.

As you sit, do not expect spiritual signs but allow the peace to enfold you and well up from your Spirit within. As your peace and stillness become even more profound through continued daily practice, you shall witness a shift in focused energies within your consciousness and an uplifting joy resonating within your heart, mind, and thoughts. Allow this Spirit-peace to transform you in its gentle touch, for your life and perception therein will surely expand as your vibrational field quickens. Allow, allow, allow!

Keep at your practice and do not judge your progress, for it is within the continued daily sitting that accumulation of energies intensifies vibrational shifts within. Practice! If you are steadfast in your commitment to yourself and your expansion, your eminent reward is assured. Be within the process, the moment, as your sitting moves into Spirit stillness and peace in ever greater degree.

As your focus of concentration moves from directed intention and takes less effort though practice, the sublime, peace-filled state will overtake you, and you shall move beyond the physical level of experience to higher, finer levels of insight, knowledge, and Spirit alignment. It is truly a scientific process of growth and expansion.

VII

*Lessons and
Exercises
to Aid in the
Quickening of
Individual Light
Vibration
Within Form*

✦

A ll of Creation upon all dimensions of being is made up of and
sustained by God's thought, and God's being is simply Light. All
is Light at varying levels of manifestation upon dimensional frequencies
and planes of being. All form, physical and otherwise, is bound by the
Divine Laws of Light, formation and structure, and the Infinite Mind can
be accessed within by the individual who is in alignment with Spirit and
the Infinite Will of the Father-God Principle.

The ability to manipulate the atomic and subatomic particles of the
physical dimension is easily accomplished by the God-man. He simply
calls upon the laws of manifestation within the God-Force Principle.
Through focused will and knowledge of Light application, he alters,
through the Light of Infinite Mind, the appropriate frequency to accomplish the desired result. All matter, being Light in density of
vibration, is therefore alterable and within the capabilities of man
aligned with God. All things are possible with knowledge of Divine Laws
of Infinite Mind. All is God; God is Light!

This chapter deals with specific exercises and lessons dealing with the
desired, focused quickening of Light vibration within form for the purpose of
awakening and altering frequencies for mankind's next step into Godhood.

The function of the human brain as an instrument of awakening is known to ancient sages and enlightened masters and is used for attaining heightened stages of consciousness. As these exercises are practiced, the brain capacity will correspondingly activate certain centers and glandular secretions to open up dormant areas. The human brain was meant to function at full capacity, yet the normal man uses less than ten percent of his capacity.

A mastermind, one who is enlightened within his being, utilizes those brain centers in much greater degree, sometimes operating at the full one-hundred-percent capacity. He has learned about the connection between body, mind, and Spirit and those areas of perception which operate through glandular psychic activation in the brain.

Here we see that breathing and breath control play a large part in the physiological activation of brain centers and states of awareness. As breath is directed and focused upon certain rhythmic patterns of control, these centers are literally awakened from their dormant state. They are brought into operation to be used to aid the aspirant in increasing Light vibration frequencies in physical cellular levels so that one may literally raise himself up to levels of vibration beyond the physical structure and formation of physical reality.

As the breath is brought under direct control, thought patterns shift and mind activity becomes clarified and focused. Subsequent infiltration of higher octaves of Light frequency alter and adjust chemical output of glandular secretions, thereby bringing the consciousness into a greater balance of heightened awareness. Body, mind, and Spirit become more aligned, and the union of integration takes place on physical and etheric levels of being. This brings into fruition the manifestation of enlightened mind states.

The ancient yogis knew much of the inner developmental states brought on by the proper use of breath and meditative practices and held this knowledge to be quite sacred. They allowed only those chosen initiates, or chelas, access to the secret practices and teachings. They guarded the passage of sacred information quite closely and offered that teaching or practice only when the disciple was fully prepared through preliminary purification and self-discipline. The master yogi would instruct his disciples on the use and application of these breathing techniques while keeping a close eye on their progress and personal unfoldment. Only when the master felt they were ready would he impart the greater secret of breath control for, to the unprepared initiate, the usage of these powerful techniques would prove harmful, both mentally and physically. If not properly done, they could have disastrous results. Therefore, the wisdom and knowledge of a master were quite necessary for the evolving disciple, and complete trust was given unto the master for his spiritual training.

At the time of transformation, the use and application of breathing techniques are still necessary under the watchful eye of the master teacher. In this book, we feel it appropriate to give only those exercises of breath which would not be seen as harmful, even if improperly applied. We would suggest, however, that there are those systems of evolutionary advancement of breath technique to be explored by the desirous aspirant if he so wills and desires.

The term "Kriya" refers to an advanced breathing technique taught by the Self-Realization Fellowship established by the great modern yogi, Paramahansa Yogananda. They offer this technique under proper guidance in safety and self-preparation.

This book is not meant to deal with specific techniques of breath control as each reader and student needs the wise guidance of one who is adept at this and who can guide him step by step while viewing his daily progress in a controlled situation. The acquisition of altered mind states through breathing is best done under this guidance.

Each aspirant, through personal desire for upliftment, must come to this knowledge in proper time, if it is their path to do so, and discover the results for themselves through daily discipline and practice.

The lessons we give can be easily practiced by all readers. They will produce wondrous results if properly applied in your daily lives. The activation and expansion of Light frequency is the goal of these practices and lessons, and each of you must prove for yourself the validity and truth of them through the results you achieve in every level of life. In truth, all spiritual practices have to work with every aspect of being if the student is to realize success and come to the ultimate awareness of his oneness with Spirit. Let us begin.

Practices and Exercises

Lesson 1 — Be in the Now

Be aware in the now! Focus your attention upon all that is transpiring within yourself on as many levels as possible. For example, as you are working, playing, in activity, instead of allowing thoughts to focus haphazardly and out of alignment with present-moment awareness, seek to simply "be" in whatever activity or action you are undertaking. When walking, direct your awareness and say to yourself, "walking." When eating, reflect "eating." It is simple, yet the mind needs constant vigilance to bring it back to center and the now because it is undisciplined and seeks to wander aimlessly from past programming to future expectations. Practice through simple exercise in all that you do and you shall perceive a greater focus of awareness developing within you as well as heightened perceptual capabilities.

Lesson 2 — Meditate! Meditate! Meditate!

Find a suitable method of stilling the body and mind in meditation and practice it daily. This is the surest way to align your vibrational field with incoming Light frequencies. In the stillness of yourself, God is known. "Be still and know that I am God."

Lesson 3 — Visualize Your Own Light

Practice seeing yourself as Spirit-Light emanating within and beyond your body form. Practice the presence of Spirit, constantly reminding yourself that you are limitless Light, not bound to past fears or beliefs, but free, emancipated from the earthly laws of limitation. Your thoughts and mind shall set you free, so direct your thoughts to concepts of unlimitedness, unconditional Love, and infinite acceptance of yourself as you are now, this very day.

Lesson 4 — Laugh and Be of Good Cheer

Play and laugh in the Lightness of your being for the density of vibrational emotions such as guilt, depression, or fear only bind you to the heaviness of lower thought forms and tie you up to the karmic chain of illusion even more. God is laughter, so be God, be laughter, be Light. See the humor in the comedy of life, see the wondrous joke of it all, and realize that nothing is so serious or so overwhelming that the laughter from realizing that you are God cannot override the illusion of fear, pain, and temporary dramas you have created for yourself. The Divine Comedy laughs with you as well, because inwardly "all know they are but dreaming."

Lesson 5 — Strengthen the Body through Proper Nutrition

Eat lightly and drink plenty of fresh water. Consume vegetables, fruits and nuts. Try to eliminate heavy foods such as meat, dairy products, sweets, and salts. Be aware of what you put into your temple. Seek to nourish your body and mind by proper habits of physical care.

Lesson 6 — Practice Fasting Once a Week

Take one day out of the week and eat nothing. Drink as much water as you would like, but do not take any solid food into your body. This will help prepare you and cleanse the organs and internal systems to allow greater Light frequencies to alter cellular and subcellular atomic patterns within the physical body.

Lesson 7 — Use a System of Stretching or Yoga

Begin to get in touch with your body temple with stretching or yoga techniques to strengthen your body's elasticity and its immune system. This will aid in bringing in greater perception of altered states as well because it will align the various glandular, endocrine, and nervous systems in proper balance of health and harmony so that the greater work of self-realization within form can be accomplished.

Lesson 8 — Learn to Flow

Relax and learn to flow with the rhythm of Nature's pace. Be attentive to your own speed and comfortable flow within self to align with those Light frequencies with greater ease and compatibility. Move more slowly. See the sky. Smell the roses. Touch the Earth. Feel the joy in simplicity within self.

Lesson 9 — Love Yourself

The single most important exercise and practice is to realize and regard yourself with the greatest honor and respect because you are God. Loving yourself is practicing the presence of Spirit, for it is exclaiming to the world that you have accepted the God within and Love all that you are in the perfection of yourself now, in this moment, thus allowing all the good, all the Love, all the vibrational quickening necessary to lift you up to God's loving arms and the great purpose and destiny to be fulfilled for yourself.

Lesson 10 — Ask for Help and Guidance

Pray and ask for guidance in all things as the higher powers that be are ready and willing to aid you in all that you do to accelerate your growth and evolution. Your guides and teachers desire that you ask for their help because it also serves their destiny to be of service to you. Do not be afraid to ask for any and all things and then be faithful and patient in the response. Spirit has its own methods and times of delivery so do not limit the gift through expectation of particular results.

Lesson 11 — Follow Your Heart

In all things, follow your heart, follow your inner voice because it is your God-self beckoning you forward in Love for your own greatest good and learning. Seek always to align yourself with the ways of your heart, for in its wisdom, it shall lead you on to your destiny in perfection. Know that your heart shall never lead you astray but is to be trusted as the voice of God unto you.

Accept and follow these simple lessons and you shall experience the quickening of higher-dimensional alteration and the expanding Light frequencies in ever greater degree daily. Do not be concerned with your progress but instead with your ever-evolving love and acceptance of yourself, now and always.

VIII

♦

*The Creation of
the
Omnidimensional
Body and its
Subsequent Use*

♦

The omnidimensional body is basically one formed through higher-consciousness application. It is created to allow one access to unlimited dimensional alteration. When used properly, it facilitates the higher-self connection to oversoul properties and information of celestial order in addition to complete freedom of movement and expression in physical as well as subtler dimensions of being. The conscious focus of sustained thought is the key to formation and materialization.

Using properties of subtle vibratory elements (lifetrons), the higher-consciousness centers also resonate, lift, and quicken the physical elemental atomic vibrations through Divine Will. Thus, the term "ascension," whereby one lifts through Love (focused thought-force projection) the vibrational frequency into higher and greater movement until physical properties become unseen in physical matter, transmuting atomic particles and subatomic particles into the frequency of Light.

By conscious and superconscious thought and Divine Will, one is directed to whatever dimension or area (either physical or nonphysical) and to whatever entity or spirit is needed for service and growth. The use and application of this skill is invaluable when moving from dimension to dimension and is gained only by selfless service, Divine Grace, and cosmic attunement, or connective consciousness, to the purposes and will of All That Is. One never can use this for personal gain or aggrandizement because the higher order of beings and universal mind will not allow it. The vibratory Creation and realms therein are created under universal harmony and universal law. Although the angelic and superconscious realms and beings therein may move into lower frequencies of denser vibrations, those whose consciousness limits their awareness may not move to higher, more subtle realms unless and until they have sufficiently grown and realized their own God-self connection and have expanded their perception of realities beyond preconception. This results in the division of worlds, the boundaries of dimensional vibration and Creation, the many mansions of God's Love and unlimited kingdoms within His being.

It is now, at these transitional times, that this knowledge should be gained by those willing to make the choice for Light and for God's purpose and plan to unfold upon and within the minds of men and the heart of Humanity. In days to come, we shall reveal in great detail the collective skills which you and others possess in this work, and how to access this information in physical dimension from others with whom you will make connection.

You may also create this omnidimensional body while outside of your physical body, independent of the physical system for travel in other worlds and dimensions. You may form the body through thought and materialize it using the same system of lifetron and positron particles manifesting the likeness of your choice, whatever that may be, in whatever form pleases you. The advantage of developing the skill of "taking the physical body along" is great because once gained, one is no longer at the mercy of matter and the transition of physical death.

Death, in fact, becomes meaningless as this vibratory application supersedes the necessity for the soul to leave the worn-out encasement. Through this application and knowledge, disease and old age become easily transmutable and thus useless in the realization of self. The soul is no longer bound by karmic restrictions and is free to come and go at will. In the age to come, many will acquire this knowledge and apply it, thus eliminating the system of karmic rebirth and reincarnation unless it pleases them to incarnate in other bodies, either on this planet or in other physical systems, for the purpose of greater growth. Yet, it is not necessary unless one chooses to do so. Once this state is reached, the karmic lessons are learned and the chains of experience are broken, thereby allowing the advancement of being in greater degree to accomplish the greater purpose without the unnecessary wheel of rebirth.

There have been many upon your plane who have achieved this, and many more are currently in preparation for this. Part of our work is training to awaken the latent knowledge of interdimensional transmutation and travel so that this knowledge is brought forth more rapidly at this time. Your planet is soon to change its appearance in vast proportions. There are those who shall lead great numbers of souls to safety and areas of greater awareness in troubled days of disruption. There are those who, in their deeper selves, know this and many other things to come. There are those who shall be as beacons of light in the dark night of fear and confusion. Their purpose is clear; their strength is sure. They are placed in certain areas, many of them for this work. As they awaken to their full purpose, their power and awareness shall prove to be of great value in days to come.

In accessing the properties of manifesting, the cellular alteration of vibration to coalesce and regroup in higher frequency states is accomplished through the act of will in cosmic alignment with Spirit. As the focus of intent and mind is brought masterfully under control and is directed in one-pointed fashion upon the heightening of vibrational Light frequency within subcellular and atomic particles within the physical system, the heightened perceptual vibratory rate quickens as the God-Force Principle and knowledge therein come into play to enact the material shift from physical matter to Light properties. As the physical atomic and subcellular or cellular levels move more swiftly, they adjust their frequency within the quickening as the will and focused thought are brought into greater alignment with Spirit energies. The Light particles which form the material properties of the physical body begin to resonate and vibrate at higher and higher levels until the physical structure is raised in vibrational capacity to the point of Light, thereby rendering it unseen in the physical through visual sensory means. Thus, at this faster vibratory rate, the vehicle becomes omnidimensionally mobile and can be utilized to access other frequencies of reality and dimensional planes. As the accessing of these various levels of dimensional vibration is achieved, the entity moves beyond third-dimensional laws and enters the realm of unlimited capabilities and understanding. The formulation of the omnidimensional body through this expanded awareness is truly the means of travel for future-past exploration as the timelessness and spacelessness characteristics of universal design are seen for what they are. The omnidimensional traveler is free to explore worlds of wonder and awe, gaining access to wisdom's heights while still retaining a body of form, fully able to alter its vibrational pattern and to shift to dimensional character on each succeeding plane or level therein. As one moves from level to level, one learns and expands into the infinite winds of timeless understanding and becomes more of that which one truly is — the God-Force Principle. The mastermind, fully conscious and aware of this process of travel and interdimensional form alteration, is liberated from space and time principles and can function on various multidimensional levels simultaneously, with full conscious awareness. The capabilities become unlimited in this state, and the design of God-man functioning as Spirit, free to choose and partake of the endless kingdoms of God's universal Creation, becomes fully realized. This is what awaits you, oh Humanity, as your birth into Light and into God-self begins and comes to be so. So be it.

IX ✦

In the Aftermath of the Dawn of Spirit

✦

Envision a world wherein all beings are taught from childhood the ways of truth and the understanding of Spirit. Imagine that all of mankind knows its oneness with all of Creation and experiences abilities far beyond those presently used. Picture an environment in which everyone is safe within the knowledge of their endless existence within God's loving heart, and in which everyone shares in the Light of the creative aspects of equality on all levels. Close your eyes and view the vast, collective energies of a Humanity united in purpose and higher thought, extending its conscious application of inner truth outward into the world in laughter, trust, and honesty. Picture this and you shall receive but a glimpse of that which awaits you and all of Humanity in your near future, a future that lies but a breath away in your time, in the aftermath of Spirit.

It is but a short duration upon Terra until the full focus of energies unites the collective universal mind in oneness of purpose and fully awakens the majority of mankind to its unification in Spirit. Man currently is still unaware, for the most part, of that which is upon him and which awaits him. Yet, collectively, man feels and knows deep within that great change and great promise beckon at his doorstep and knock upon the door of his consciousness for entry and residence therein. It is still calling in the caverns of his soul and swiftly comes forward with a voice that grows louder and clearer with each passing moment. Your reality, oh Humanity, is soon to alter, and your perception of yourself is to expand into the limitlessness of God's eternal presence within you.

Spirit is awakening you from your sleep of illusion and shaking you from your dream. Soon you shall bear witness to vast transformation upon Terra in every aspect of her land and form. You shall view the uplifting of Humanity into Light and into his true destiny.

As the full force and intensity of the higher vibratory quickening is in place throughout all of material Creation, and individual consciousness has been illuminated, darkness shall be no more. You shall walk, live, laugh, and sing in Light. Through that Light, your world and everything in it shall be transformed into something vastly beyond all that you could possibly imagine in this present moment. It will be something so incredibly joy-filled that your interpretation and concept of all that is good, all that is of highest fulfillment, cannot compare. The "new" man, the new God-child, awakened unto himself, shall walk this plane in harmony, truth, and Love, and he shall know of his place within God's creative universe and the power which resides within his being.

In the aftermath of Spirit, after the dawn of awakening has occurred, the new day of Earth's quiet, patient potential shall be fully activated. She shall settle into her conscious place as a fully enlightened star, supporting conscious sons and daughters of God-Spirit upon her.

Fear, and its subsequent emotional-psychological imbalance, shall be replaced by the harmonic alignment of spiritual understanding realized through personal, individual experience of those Light energies of awakening and oneness with the Creator Spirit within all.

Life and its experience shall be known to be filled with hope, fullness, and joy within the nowness of Spirit's loving embrace in all that is said and done. The higher pattern of vibrational frequency shall bring new, harmonious energies of opportunity for evolving consciousness upon every plane of creative expression. The manifestation of material Creation shall be placed in Humanity's hands as the Infinite Power, understood and held by all within spiritual conscious application, shall indeed become commonplace and be used to its fullest potential, thereby ending all pain and disease within form and physical matter. The alignment of spiritual energies focused into material form shall be of such magnitude that all former patterns of vibrational frequency shall be elevated and altered to accommodate these greater frequencies. This will transform present conditions of physical experience into advanced shifts of dimensional alignment which will create quantum leaps in consciousness into forth- and fifth-dimensional accessibility and communication. This will also elevate awareness with inter- and extraterrestrial forms and dimensions. The boundaries and limitations of thought consciousness shall be a thing of the past and the freedom of the soul's oneness with Infinite Universal Mind shall reign in its place.

Man, in oneness with his brothers, shall create a unified, harmonious playground of Spirit upon Terra with new and unparalleled vistas of Light. Peace-filled concepts shall be taught to all incarnate souls. Children shall be properly seen and understood as being ageless sparks of God's united being. They shall no longer be taught limitation or fear. They shall be allowed total freedom to express their creative potential in the knowledge of their oneness with all Creation. Higher-consciousness application and the Laws of Harmony and Light shall make up the educational curriculum communicated and taught by elders and the collective communities of Light beings in connection with interdimensional and extradimensional intelligence for the purpose of evolutionary advancement of Spirit principles. Tools and techniques of dimensional travel via the omnidimensional body and dematerialization, as well as physical materialization, shall be widely known. Eventually, it will become the norm as individual expansion culminates in final and complete mastery over material Creation.

The heightened, intense power of thought at one with the dynamic principles of Higher Will shall indeed create instantaneously all desired objects and experiences to manifest in material form. Lower life forms shall be seen no longer as "lower" but as equal. They will be cherished contributors to the whole of evolving consciousness and therefore shall be preserved and cared for with equal regard for all by all. Communication with animals and all other species shall be accomplished through thought. Vast new knowledge and understanding shall be gained through interspecies communication. As the limitations of understanding are put aside, greater forms of communication skills shall be learned since the barrier of time and space concepts shall be seen clearly as past illusion. Learning shall be experienced through connecting in consciousness with past and future aspects of yourself, not only in dream states but upon conscious awareness in clear receptivity. Love, in its true, unconditional state, shall be freely shared, felt and known as the primary motivating energy within all. Love shall be accessed to propel the advanced stages of God-man to yet further dimensions of unlimitedness.

Oh Humanity, upon you now is but the birthing process of your dawn of awakening in consciousness and revelation. Awaiting you is your maturity in full — total awareness of your Divine purpose and mastery of physical Creation. Take up your heritage, take up your power, open yourself to the greater knowingness of your oneness with All That Is and the responsibility of that knowledge. The fleeting dream of your historical process is indeed waning and shall soon be no more as your feet step out into a new world, a new millennium of Love, Light, and Spirit. Walk boldly into your now. Be present in God's presence. Clearly see your freedom as it beckons you forward in truth, in oneness, and in Love.

Oh Humanity, you are God, and soon you shall know it!

X

◆

Attachment and
Desire

◆

Throughout all of thy lives of incarnation upon form, your desire and attachment therein has propelled you back, lifetime upon lifetime, to experience and re-experience those desires and their fulfill-ment within physicality. It is those very desires and attachments that bind you to the realm of form and prevent you from seeing your truth in totality in Spirit. Whatever the attachment may be — possessions, relationships, etc. — your experience shall be limited by the role you perform and the perception of yourself in regard to your attachment or desire.

Depending on your identification with that desire or attachment, you shall have difficulty breaking free in awareness of your truth if the desire is strong because the chains of desire forged by individual will are not easily broken. The attached mind identifies with the desired object and is blind to the true reality of greater self. When speaking of freedom and awakening to one's God-self, we must address the issues of desire and attachment because these are great binders of illusion. Their continued practice shall prevent your freedom of movement into Light.

When one moves through one's life, incarnation after incarnation, experiences are brought forth as lessons to teach the soul in order to ultimately bring it to the point of awakening where it realizes the illusion of form and regains its awareness of oneness. Yet all souls, in their long journeys, create and develop certain patterns, habits, attachments, and desires which follow them as shadows, keeping the darkness about them. When one is focused in desire for whatever the world of form has to offer, one willingly separates self from the Source, creating a wall of attachment that stands between one's eternal, knowing Light and one's own conscious awareness. Limitation arises when one's attachment locks up one's consciousness within the boundaries of desire and form, thereby closing off the current of deeper understanding.

Attachment to any object, person, thought pattern, mind-set, or lifestyle shall produce limitation because one shall be unable to view the true reality beyond the identification with that attachment. Attachments come in various ways. Attachments can relate to power, wealth, money, viewpoints, fears, dreams of future desires fulfilled, one's body and looks, possessions, or other similar things. The list is extensive. However, without those chains of attachment forged through your own desires, you would view your own freedom and fly heavenward in the joy of nonattachment and nondesire.

How may one who lives in and is part of this drama of Earth life break free of his attachments and desires for those aspects of life which seemingly provide stability, joy, and honor? How is it possible that one who is attached to many things and various patterns of behavior may perceive and alter this in order to evolve into a greater understanding of life's true purpose on Earth? What can one do to come to the realization that all that has been taught to Humanity through social acceptance is but illusion and serves to create greater confusion through the belief in that which is unreal?

This can happen by simply stilling one's mind and accepting the Spirit of the everlasting God-Principle into one's life and mind, trusting in the unseen hand of Divine Love to bring forth one's own truth from within. By lessening the focus on material things and their importance, one can create a powerful inner desire for true understanding to occur. One can place his priority on that which is lasting, unchangeable, loving, pure, and Divine. One can give his own Spirit its due within his life and time. One can bring his thoughts into Spirit's wondrous dominion, creating greater hope, peace, and fulfillment within. When one begins to grow tired of the results of nonfulfillment through ego-attached desires, one begins to long for a greater freedom from those imprisoning beliefs in the reality of physicality and sets one's sights on a more lasting, peace-filled reality within one's own heart. That is indeed the only true reality — the reality of oneself within.

The attraction of attachment is strong, however, and quite deceiving. It creates the illusion of fulfillment when, in truth, the desire merely binds the mind and thought to the world of senses and form. The temporal, ever-changing winds of material Creation can never hope to give the true permanence of peace and inner fulfillment. All things of matter come and go. They have their birth and their death, their beginning and their end, whereas your Spirit, the forever self, does not. The true reality as seen is your own being, and it is the only permanent satisfaction to be sought and gained.

When viewing yourself and turning the focus of attention inward, survey the scenery of your own desires and attachments to thoughts, things, people, or situations, and ask yourself what is the true motivation, the exact outcome, the need in self to experience all that you desire and are attached to. Honestly break down and peel away the layers of thought-illusion from the true reality of self. Perceive yourself as naked, detached, sovereign, complete, and whole, with nothing to lean upon or need.

When one stumbles about in darkness, it is natural to desire light; yet, when one in blindness does not know that he is blind, he seeks only to move within the boundaries of that which he knows and which is comfortable. Be not one who, in blindness, limits himself. Instead, always seek the greater truth, the more abundant Light, to free yourself of imprisoning attachments to that which shall surely disappear one day.

The play shall continue, the dream shall go on until your understanding is applied to your life and behavior. Through arduous self-awareness, you can see through the fantasy, the dreamlike fabric of that which is unstable and without reality.

Moving past temporal existence to view the greater dimensional awareness means reorganizing your priorities and focusing attention on that which is constant. Your personal path of unfoldment must be danced upon with a widened perception of self and a more unlimited identification with the All That Is which, in truth, you are. The past and present form of identity based upon relationship to your world of form shall indeed be left behind as your field of perception comes to include all things and all experiences as the totality of your creation, your own being. Separation in superconsciousness is nonexistent because all things are understood to be one, connected beyond form.

Nonattachment and desirelessness within normal conscious expression is difficult as long as identification with form is perceived as one's reality. The acquisition of higher states of consciousness, however, is thwarted by desire and attachment states of mind. As long as man rigidly holds on to his structure of perceptual identification, he shall not be able to gain the true understanding of self without boundaries or limits. To go beyond learned belief patterns of self-identification requires curiosity and an honest reflection of one's personal view of reality and self. The fear-based walls erected about one's self as barriers for protection, which are built upon limited concepts of what and who one thinks he is, must be seen for what they are. They are walls preventing true perception of being from becoming part of man's understanding of oneness and spiritual Light.

To allow the unfolding of consciousness expansion to take place, one simply must let go of the structured patterns of self-conceptualization in order to invite entry of the greater perceptual field. One must unlearn what has been learned in order to see beyond the limits of that which society and family have taught in order to move beyond concepts of all that he has perceived himself to be.

This is no easy task and requires constant vigilance and moment-to-moment self-awareness. This must occur in order to realize that those thoughts, words, and actions, up to this moment, have created your world, your reality, and your understanding of self. To be truly honest with yourself and your feelings is most difficult for one who has been taught to rely on outer reality for verification and validity of inner truth. The illusion becomes more confusing and complex the further we step away from ourselves and our own truth. When we do this, we give away our own power. To be truly alive, one must be truly awake!

The simplicity of inner awakening is totally profound for it bypasses all outer illusion, all sense of separateness. It brings us to the beautiful vision of ourselves as one with All That Is. This eliminates all duality and complexity while completely validating our eternal foreverness as Spirit beings.

The ego, in vying for the position of master, naturally struggles to maintain control through patterns of fear and self-doubt. In the end, it must relinquish its throne to the truth of Spirit's unending wisdom and grace as the one and only reality, the one and only master. Allowance of the process of letting go is undoubtedly the most difficult achievement for the exalted ego and personality self. To allow the shift of control over to Spirit requires great faith and trust in that which is unseen and unknown to the limited self-perception. The leap and shift must be made if the inner reality of Spirit's wise direction is to be allowed to be brought forth to man's conscious awareness in fullness and totality.

As the shift occurs, man's trust in his own inner guidance shall grow stronger and be more easily perceived as each situation or circumstance offers a new test in trust and faith in himself and his higher power, which was completely ignored for so long. As man allows yet more direction from within to guide his choices, his steps shall grow easier and become more balanced, for he shall find the path of life opening into vistas of joy never before felt or seen. With each step taken in trust, even greater Love shall be experienced, for he shall know beyond doubt the truth of his own inner joy, wisdom, and reality.

The process itself requires the initial leap of faith. When one jumps into the unknown, he shall surely be caught and arrive safely through his trust in the inner wisdom of Spirit's Divine push. As the ever-expanding and intensifying waves of Light vibration pervade and penetrate the collective field of Humanity's consciousness, the awakening of new priorities from outer illusion to inner reality shall be more commonplace. The natural order and balance within the spiritual and psychological bodies of man shall be restored to vitality, health, and well-being. In this process, the fundamental shift shall be seen to encompass the restructuring of desire-attachment principles of thought and behavior to a state of healthy alignment. Spirit's design for the truth of each being's reality shall be seen and felt within each awakened heart and mind and shall naturally flow with that truth.

When man knows, within his heart of hearts, the reality of his own power, Light, and eternal nature, how can he return to desire and attachment built upon the illusion of pain and fear? When one stands joyous, filled with the presence and Light of God's unlimitedness, how could he long for the shadows of the night which only made him cower in terror and which bound him to tormenting thoughts of eventual loss and subsequent death? He cannot, he will not, for that which awaits the Humanity of awakened consciousness is a reality forged in truth, Love, and joy. Who would choose pain over joy, or sorrow over peace?

Begin now, today, to bring into your life those thoughts and actions which shall align you with the truth of your own awakening. Choose your reality built upon the secure rock of faith in yourself, in your Light, in your God. Each moment of each day, step closer to your own personal contact with the Lord God of your being, and find your desire for that which is real speaking louder to you than the voice of desire built upon the dream of illusion. Soon the voice of illusion shall become a faint whisper which disappears in the night as the rays of Light break through the darkness, dispelling the shadows of past fears and doubts from your mind, your heart, and your life, leaving you standing naked in joy, in Love, and in God. So be it! Walk bravely forward, walk bravely inward unto yourself, oh, God-man.

XI

♦

The Gentle Way

♦

My wondrous brothers and sisters of Terra, I have come upon you to bring to you a new hope, a new understanding that there is a gentler way to live your lives in trust, in Love, and in Light. There is a gentler way to perceive yourself and your world in openness, realizing that we and all beings, are interconnected in Divine unity of Spirit, now and always. Upon the entire universe of God's thought, there is absolutely nothing to fear. You are ever safe, ever loved in the timelessness of God's being. Your consciousness shall continue to evolve to heights not dreamed of in your wildest imagination.

The gentle way begins when your heart and mind are awakened to yourself in Love, acceptance, and forgiveness. The gentle way reveals to you the joy to be found within yourself when you relinquish doubt and the fears of all that you are and instead embrace the new, the transformation of your being into the Light of knowing that you are forever, you are God!

It is neither difficult nor demanding to walk this path. All that is required is to allow the old patterns of fear and doubt to release themselves from you. You must also trust in the Divine, unlimited hand of the Father-God Principle within to direct your steps in loving gentleness. You are never alone, and your needs and desires are seen and understood by Spirit at all times during your journey.

To walk the gentle way requires only your own self-perception to awaken to Love, to know that you are loving and loved. From that premise, build upon those aspects of Divine heritage from union with the God-self.

The gentle way is one in which every aspect of your life is taken into account and lived in such focus that all is brought into harmony, balance, and self-honesty. The gentle way asks nothing of you except to be present in each of your nows and to recognize the eternal nature of the Love that you are and the expression therein.

The gentle way quietly teaches you your own truth and does not demand or expect you to be anything more than what you are within your own evolving understanding. The gentle way softly carries you upward on your journey to the door of Light and safely sets you down upon your throne of inner knowingness.

I beckon you now to let go of your fears and past patterns of self-limitation and walk the gentle way with us now so that we may aid you in your days upon Terra, and beyond, to your own eternalness within God's Infinite Kingdom.

I call out to each and every ear that hears my words to join with us in awakening all upon this plane to their own joy, Light, and truth. Will you join with us now in this great purpose?

The gentle way welcomes each and every being to enjoy the fruits of the Father's feast and to take their place in the unfolding plan of heaven on Earth. So be it.

May all of mankind awaken within their hearts to the gentle way of Spirit-oneness within.

Om. Peace. Bliss. Understanding.

XII

♦

Coming from Love

♦

Ithin Love's boundlessness, your truth is found within you, not through some false image of perfection, but upon that moment when you know within your heart of hearts that all you have placed upon the mantle of your identification in form has been but an illusion. When you truly understand this statement, you shall begin to view all of your thoughts, actions, and words in a vast new choice, a choice coming from Love. All that is upon your truth and within the truth of all Creation has its foundation and creativity coming from Love.

When we speak of coming from the Love energy within, we view the world of form and perceive the difficulty within the turbulence of your pains, sorrows, and misfortunes in connecting with and directing yourself from a loving place. We are here to help you see anew, and through the clarity of your newfound vision, truly move within your world through the emergence in Love. We communicate through you now using the higher energies of Love and those advancing frequencies therein. We seek to reveal to you those levels of yourself in Love that shall help you transform your inner and outer reality to one of great joy and happiness.

I, and those with whom I work, traverse many dimensions. We see the endless reality of Love's unlimited power and energy. We gather a small portion of this energy now in our connection with you to impart the vast aspects of opportunity you may gain when coming from Love by using this awesome energy for the good of all.

When we connect to these vast, creative vortices within worlds, the pulsating rhythm of God's thought moves within our being. We blissfully carry forth the purpose of our existence: to Love, to be Love, to express Love, and to know the Love that we are in totality of experience. Coming from Love is connecting to that endless reservoir of wondrous energy, the energy that all of Creation springs from; and feeling and knowing the creative power that is ours to use to transform all disharmony and imbalance into its true alignment with Love. This brings forth that perfection, that total oneness which we all seek to know and recognize.

As you move within and experience your reality, begin to view and imagine your world and your life completely immersed within this Love energy. See the harmony all about you in all of your moments. Create through Love, and imagine a perfect space and opportunity for all of life's wondrous connectedness to awaken to its Love, Light and joy. Clearly picture your world bathing in its own self-love, shining radiantly outward to all of Creation. Do this daily practice to counter the thought-forms of ill will and ignorance that encompass your atmosphere. You shall see a great change in your own life and experiences as you make your own reality brighter and lighter in Love's wake.

Coming from Love is allowing the truth of each individual consciousness to be exactly what it is without judgment or conditions of limitation. Coming from Love is seeing the intricate patterns of all of universal Creation tied together in a tapestry of remarkable beauty and glory beyond concepts or beliefs. Coming from Love is completely accepting yourself in each now of your experience, and allowing yourself to express the perfection of your being in all ways, without critical thought or expectation.

The allowance of creative, spontaneous expression through Love is indeed being your higher self and recognizing the union of your soul with God's Light and joy. The Father-God Principle is ever playful, ever spontaneous in his creativity. His laughter fills the universe of Love's tender being, sending waves of joy throughout all of eternity.

Coming from Love is coming from the heart, the heart of the One Spirit within, and touching other hearts in unity of God's purpose and peace. Loving yourself is the first step home; loving all else is the way, the path; and being Love is the journey's end, for once you become that which you are — Love — you shall truly be home within your Father's arms.

XIII ✦

The Common Bond

✦

We are joined with you now in all your choices and undertakings as we bring our message to your world of form in the hope that all upon Terra will soon awaken from their sleep of darkness and know the great joy to be found in their own Light.

We share a common bond with all of mankind for we were once as you are, stumbling in the ignorance of illusion, lost within the dream of false ego attachment, and unaware of our own divinity within. Yet, we awoke to self-realization of our union with God and, verily, so shall you and all of Humanity one day. We share the common bond of Love and understanding with you and come to you as guides for your journey home to God's Kingdom within. We reach out to all of your brethren in humility and honesty to share our truth with you, to reveal a greater hope, and to light a candle that will spark others to shine their radiance upon the darkness of your world, on and on until one day all of this plane shall shine its Light, its Love, and its unity of the common bond all share.

As we speak, we understand the difficulty of many individuals to grasp all that we have to impart. There is difficulty, as well, to convince mankind of the existence of life-intelligences outside of three-dimensional form and physicality, yet we persist, for our purpose is sure. We seek not to convince, but to love you into this awakening. To spend the vast amount of energy it would take just to convince many of your brothers of our existence is, in fact, pointless, for he who refuses to believe shall not accept possibilities outside of the limited walls he has erected about his mind. Our mission is much more important than pursuing the path of parlor tricks or manipulation to bring about the trust of Humanity. We never could or would do this for it is each entity's choice as to their reality, belief, and acceptance of self-knowledge.

We, instead, walk the gentle way of revealing our Light and truth to all who desire it, and we lovingly share the bond with all. We seek to create this common bond, not only in understanding and accepting our reality, but by invoking this understanding within man's common bond with all of life and intelligence therein. In order for man to advance to the next step on his evolutionary path, he must come to this understanding of life's Eternal Presence within universal Creation, and he must bond with All That Is in this knowingness.

XIV ✦

The Wonderment
of Being

✦

U pon the platform of desire, Humanity has created for itself a
myriad of complexities designed in illusion, with the subconscious
hope of fulfillment and satisfaction at the end. Yet, as one desire
becomes fulfilled, the entity realizes that ultimate fulfillment still eludes
him, and so he sets up for himself another challenge, another goal to
reach. In the long struggle for self-understanding, each being must
come to the final awareness that all action and outer searching for life's
purpose is futile because all truth resides within our own self. The
dream of illusion continues as long as the consciousness places focus
upon extraneous goals outside of the truth of self. In reality, if all beings
would but glimpse their own Light, they would be astonished to realize
that they are already perfect and Divine, and that there is absolutely
nothing to achieve outside of the recognition of the wonderment of
being.

Society has taught that each entity must work, must struggle to
achieve, must slave for success at the expense of inner exploration and
the value of a more peace-filled, harmonious approach to daily life. The
masses are taught that in order to be successful, one must deny oneself
time for relaxation and regeneration; that time not applied to one's
career or the acquisition of wealth is lost and wasted time and, therefore,

unproductive and illogical.

The psyche of the individual experiences mounting pressure and stress which ultimately results in a breakdown of health in mind and body. Modern man must come to the realization that, in the greater picture, he places this upon himself through his beliefs and programming. In the final analysis, the only true requirement of his gaining true success in living is in simply being.

There are no timetables within Love. There is no master to serve. There is no pressure or stress other than that which man creates in his own reality. In truth, once perceived, the Spirit flies free of all limits, all boundaries, and one begins to live in the moment, in the now, without demanding anything more of life than just "to be," simply, and with joy.

Part of the ego's demands for satisfaction rests in the Creation of challenges or problems to be overcome in order to strengthen its hold and position upon the consciousness. If the ego could see that Spirit is its true ally, friend, and sole supplier of all things good, it would at once relinquish its hold and allow Divine intervention to take place, thus freeing the consciousness to reach higher states of being and perception.

The wonderment of being is the true, harmonious state for all awakened consciousness, and that which awaits Humanity shortly, but the task at hand is to pave the way for a smoother transition from ego control to spiritual freedom. We seek to allay fears of enslavement and belief patterns of hopelessness within man's framework of understanding. We wish to reveal the emancipating truth within each individual and the collective consciousness. Each of you must realize firsthand your own power and Light if change is to occur smoothly within the quickening of higher vibratory influence.

The concept of "being" essentially suggests that harmony and fulfillment truly come from within. All that is necessary is for the individual to "be." This allows the process of unfoldment to take place within and about himself in alignment with the flow of Love and inner joy. This way of life does not mean to imply that all should drop what they are doing, sit back on their laurels, and become lackadaisical in their lives.

On the contrary, in assuming this state, each entity must be completely aware of himself in the moment in order to allow the process of Spirit to flow. It may sound like a dichotomy but indeed it is not, for the lazy individual is unaware of himself and his purpose, whereas the individual who resides in the now is totally aware and present. He does not seek to manipulate and control all things outside of himself, but instead allows all things to be as they are, allows all individuals to express the totality of their experience, allows life to unfold while enjoying the process as an observer would enjoy a film or play being enacted.

The wonderment of being is in its simplicity. It is freeing to the individual because it speaks of a gentler way of experiencing the miracle called life. It calls to the child in each of us to let go of the rigidity of living in self-created stress and pressure. It encourages us to revel in the play of our lives as little children exploring the world in laughter and joy. It seeks to remind us of the simple approach, to bring us home to the understanding that all Love, all happiness is to be found within our own being by simply "being," without expectation of anything other than what we, ourselves, can give.

To "be" means to be present, aware, fully conscious of all that is taking place within us each moment, and to flow with ourselves effortlessly as the unfolding experience of life's current carries us upward in Love and joy. The more consciously aware one is, the easier it becomes to allow the process of being to take place and to release the demands of ego for certain outcomes or to control experiences. We simply flow with the direction of Spirit's song within us. In its unfailing wisdom, it creates a beautiful harmony within our lives never before found or heard. We begin to trust in the process of "being" and let the past patterns of fear and self-doubt fall by the wayside, thus allowing ourselves even more joy and peace.

To come to the full realization that in all of life there is nothing one has to be but oneself is quite emancipating; yet being oneself has significantly different connotations to most beings when they are in the dreamlike fabric of illusion. When seen from the perspective of Spirit, however, being oneself is all there is. In its complete simplicity, it means being Love, Light, and endless essence. When one is a master of being, he is a master of life, for he views all experiences as a reflection of Spirit-self in motion and is able to be himself each moment in harmony and joy, no matter what is occurring in the outer dream of seeming reality.

The wonderment of being is a joyous realization on every level of life because it reveals the greater reality of Love in actualization within us and its infinite potential activated in the nowness of our lives. We are Love, and in the wonder of now, we are fully able to be that Love in totality, and then to express it in its purest aspect of innocence to all we see and touch. To be is all that is required of ourselves. It is the joyous, loving expression of our Spirit-selves in complete freedom, complete joy, and complete perfection.

Therefore, allow yourself to relax with the flow of your own Divine being, and take joy in the awareness of yourself, at one with peace, at one with life, at one with God, now and forever.

XV

✦

The Angelic
Presence

✦

As the vibratory waves of Light interpenetrate the field of Terra and all of matter's frequencies, the dimensional walls which separate Humanity's consciousness and third-dimensional awareness from higher fourth- and fifth-dimensional connection become less dense. Riding the crest of these waves of Light unto mankind's awareness as a forerunner of destiny is the mighty and wondrous Love of the Angelic Presence. These messengers of Divine calling come now, in numbers greater than this dimension has ever known, to herald the kingdom of God's purpose on Earth to all. Their presence is felt and known in all walks of life now, and their power is truly awesome as they move upon and within your world of form. They bring Light, laughter and blissful feelings into the world. Do not be surprised at the stranger who stands beside you beaming with silent understanding, or the sweet babe who stares deeply into your eyes with wisdom's knowing. No, do not be surprised, for these very well might be angelic messengers of Light who have come to point a clearer way to your being during these times of transition. These wondrous beings of angelic vibration fly swiftly now unto this plane of manifestation and carry forth their great plan of deliverance to all who are open and longing for greater connection to the Light of God-knowingness.

In higher, grander perceptivity, these beings are truly magnificent to behold as they radiate golden rays of Light outward in all directions, altering fields of receptive communication within man's consciousness. The higher call has gone out and they have answered with their mighty presence, here and now. They are in the process of aiding each individual consciousness to awaken gently to the path of Love. They come to offer assistance within various tasks and purposes according to each situation presented. They will bring comfort and guidance as they allow their presence to be felt. Do not hesitate to ask for their assistance in any and all situations for they are bound to the cause of unfoldment and stand ready to call forth all that is necessary to achieve that end within Humanity's awakening.

The angelic kingdom, in purity of vibration, excels and adds its harmonious Love to help bridge the frequency of matter in connectivity to the greater frequencies of Spirit's interdimensional realms so that Humanity will indeed be able to walk and talk, hand in hand, with the angelic kingdoms of Light in full awareness. They bring with them celestial songs of such grand, harmonious magnitude that, in their presence, deep healing and releasing occurs within psychological and emotional levels of those who are blessed by their connection.

As their music is felt, emotions well up as if from nowhere and flow upward through your being to serve as a catalyst for expansion and change. The Divine Dance of Creation plays upon the melody as the celestial soundstream carries the consciousness to heights of wonder and awe. As they align their wondrous vibration with Terra's expanding energies, they move within form and consciousness of those individuals who allow and attune to receive the blessings which they have to offer. Always expressing the laughter and joy of their unconditionally loving presence, they infuse each open entity with hope and promise of fulfillment. They also act as agents of manifestation to create those desired wishes of a consciousness united in Love with the Father Principle. They are the harbingers of peace and stand ever ready to fulfill the plan of the Father-God Spirit in any and all situations.

To feel or align with their presence takes only your open, trusting heart and mind, in honesty and Love, asking in humility for their connection.

"Ask and ye shall receive; knock and the door shall be opened unto thee."

Whatever you should require, whatever problems or challenges face you, you need only to ask for help, and you shall receive it at every step of your journey to take you safely home to God's doorstep. Allow Spirit and the Angelic Presence to make clear your path so your steps flow with grace, beauty and ease. Be faithful in their presence, and trust that all is taken care of to smooth the road before you.

You may feel their presence in the melody of a song, in the smile of a baby, in the eyes of a stranger, or in the wind as it caresses your face. You may feel their presence near you by the thrill of vibrational quickening traveling up your spine, by a rush of energy in your head, or by a tingling sensation which feels as if tiny fingers were tickling your very soul with their laughter, Love, and Light.

Be aware, for they appear at any given moment as they are directed by the Father Principle. They come and go as their tasks are completed. Be open to their voices of Love and melody, and from within you shall you hear the celestial choir sing music so beautiful that your being shall be uplifted and carried to worlds of wonder beyond anything you have known. Hasten their arrival into your life through your humble purity in heart and your honest intent to be a candle burning in the night to all other souls who hunger for Love, who long for understanding. If you focus your steps on the path of service to your fellow men, the great forces of angelic splendor shall serve you, bowing at your feet in honor, respect, and obedience. If you turn your thoughts to aid in the upliftment of Humanity's hope and faith, the heavens of angelic splendor shall fill the ethers with God's praise and Love as the universal melodies flow forth, fulfilling the Divine Plan and purpose for man.

Be the Light, be the Love, and share your wondrous bounty with all who connect with you in life. Demonstrate your Spirit and your Light to all. Be the beacon who guides the ships lost in the density of darkness to the safe shores of God's grace and peace through your Light and knowingness. Be the fulfillment of all that the Father-God Principle intended you to be in all of your days, in all of the ways, and discover the bliss of wholeness with the All That Is. Join the choir of voices as the Angelic Presence unites with matter in these times of transformation. Sing clearly, sing gently the song of yourself, the song of your Love, the song of your Spirit-God. Laugh with the angels, and hear the universal Father's laughter ringing in your ears, bringing joy, bliss and fulfillment to your soul.

XVI ✦

Becoming Empty

✦

Imagine yourself as a vase or urn filled to overflowing with the beliefs, images, and concepts in all their complexity of your human intellectual reasoning. You have gorged upon the past patterns of subconscious behavior and ideology, thus creating no space or room for the quiet, gentle grace of Spirit-consciousness to enter.

Consider for a moment yourself in all of this as a vase which must empty itself in order to allow the simple purity of Spirit's frequency to enter and flow unimpeded throughout the various levels and sublevels of your heart, mind, and life. This is truly what must be done for the new awareness, the expanded God-Consciousness, to become part of and one with your being in total comprehension. You have taken upon yourself, in untold incarnations, much complexity, dross, and misguided beliefs which prevent you from experiencing the fullness of God's presence within you.

"Except ye be as little children, ye shall not enter the Kingdom of Heaven."

Unless you unlearn all that you have learned, unless you become as empty urns ready to receive anew all that is of Spirit, you shall not be able to perceive the grandeur of your own being, the spectacle of your God-self. Your concepts of intellectual, human reasoning; your practical approach to your own life through limited, fearful perceptions of your reality and the world; and your beliefs in all your extravagant, myriad confusions merely act as barriers to the childlike simplicity of faith and trust in the God of your being. To become as little children is a most profound truth. It moves directly to the heart of simplicity and innocence without the weight of fearful, limiting concepts of self. A child can merely be, can simply view the moment, can play in the trusting purity of Love's ways, enjoying each now, each moment without the rigidity or the inflexible thought patterns which, through fear and self-doubt, leave the man of maturity or intellectual reasoning but a fixed, inert consciousness, afraid to move forward for fear of oblivion or the unknown. A child lives, Loves, and accepts unconditionally the trusting hand each moment extends and is flexible in the thrust of change.

Be as the children. Empty yourself of all that you have perceived to be real, true, and of value in your human affairs and concepts. Accept the ever-expansive hand of the Father-Spirit Principle in your mind and heart. Allow the transition of Light frequencies now flooding your dimension to alter and uplift your life and consciousness. Let go of your rigid beliefs which prevent the greater concept of unlimitedness to align with you in wholeness and in balance.

Reflect upon your thoughts, your life, and those areas which hold you back and limit your free self from becoming all that you can be. Let those thoughts and beliefs dissolve in the Light of truth as the warm sun of Love melts the hardened ice of fixed concepts and fears in the new day of spring. Let them go the way of all dreams, disappearing in the morning's rising wakefulness and awareness.

As they go and the vase of your being is empty and open, you shall experience the gateway of Spirit's opening into your life and your mind. It will flood your being with Love, Light, and joy beyond anything you have known, transforming your world into a heavenly paradise of grand beauty and wonder.

Become empty of your dross. Peel away the layers of useless, illusionary identity with your thoughts of limitation. Become aware of yourself in each moment, relaxing into your own truth and childlike flow of innocent trust, and you shall surely find your way home in Love's safety, perfection and truth.

Becoming empty is indeed a paradox within your worldly view of all that is real, for it suggests that all you have been taught is of no avail and no import and must be cast aside. Your view of reality, however, has been limited to your experiences and belief system which have prevented you from seeing the clear, simple picture of your own, expanded self. We are not implying that all knowledge gained is without value, but we are saying that the degree of value placed upon the rigid thought structures which limit the natural flow of life's wonder within your consciousness is the impediment to your self-understanding. All that you have learned is not to be considered useless trash but simply to be set aside in your quest for greater knowledge of wisdom's ways within you. We do not suggest that the intellect be ignored or shut down but that you restructure the priority of importance placed on it in lieu of the greater Spirit-self. The intellect, in all its wondrous ways, could never hope to identify or quantify the immensity of knowingness and infinite perfection which your higher Spirit-self incorporates.

Becoming your highest self, in alignment with God's energy and sublime wisdom, is the greatest achievement one can accomplish while in physical form. The fruition of this oneness in consciousness moves far beyond the borders of intellectual undertaking, encompassing the total awareness of life's purpose. Yet, if your intellect is given priority as master of your life and choices, you shortchange yourself, for you do not allow yourself to see and partake of the greater possibilities which the union with your God-self offers.

Stay in your concepts and fears and you remain in darkness. Become empty and allow the influx of Love's beauteous now into your life, and you shall flow harmoniously into the Light of knowingness.

The choice is yours. In truth, who would choose sorrow over joy, darkness over Light? The seedling does not fear its growth into the mighty oak, so fear not your expansion into your unlimited self. Be courageous in your quest. Be fearless in your love. Be empty in your trust, and allow the dawn of awakening to free you from the chains of past patterns of fear so that you may walk knowingly forward into greater horizons of vast possibilities. So be it.

Walk on, oh Humanity. Walk on in the Light of Love and in the Light of truth.

XVII ✦

From Revelation

to

Superconsciousness

✦

As man's consciousness opens and exceeds previous limits of structured belief and thought, the influx of higher levels of perception and inspiration shall give way to revealing experience. Man shall receive those energies of Light vibration which shall produce the transformation of his soul into a state of oneness. Revelation is the onset, the beginning of the true state of oneness. It is characterized by the doors of intuitive insight being flung wide open, thereby allowing entry of those higher vibratory frequencies of truth, Love, and Light to filter into conscious awareness and become part of and adjacent to man's normal daily perception and thought. As the revealing experience takes place through moments of stillness and openness, man's entire perceptive field expands and alters, bringing forth quickened vibrational and dimensional properties to his reality. This allows his awareness to transcend the illusion of space and time and bestow upon him those peace-filled, joyous states which the revealing experience inspires.

As each experience carries with it those properties and qualities of expansion and cellular vibratory transmutation, man moves forward toward the permanent level of superconsciousness or God-consciousness wherein he becomes the revelation, the God which he already is, in full conscious awareness, upon every level of wholeness. This superconscious state is the result of the revelation experience. As each series of limits is met and transcended, they become viewed for what they are in actuality — discarded layers of illusion. As each limitation is released, one's feet are firmly placed in faith and trust upon the solid rock of the unfolding superconscious state. As each entity opens more to his ever-flowing Light, each shall move from revelation to superconsciousness and join in the collective harmony of the expression and expansion of God upon Terra, acting as beacons of wondrous Light, leading others to the reflection of their God-selves within. Revelation and superconsciousness equal "clarity," just as a pool of water in stillness without motion is viewed as clear, allowing one to see into its depths the treasure stored safely therein.

Revelation moves upon wings of quiet grace when your mind is free of senseless prattle (useless thoughts, fears, and desires), your heart is in peaceful receptivity, and you allow Spirit's wondrous power to flow unimpeded as waves upon the shore of your soul. Revelation is the Hand of God's infinite storehouse of knowledge knocking upon the door of your life, begging entry in those moments of oneness and openness. It is the sweet kiss of the Divine bringing forth the allness of its Love to your aching heart, revealing the greater understanding of your eternal nature. It is the gentle Spirit beckoning you to remember your heritage and power within God's kingdom of selfhood and is-ness.

Revelation is the taste of foreverness, the first steps of your childlike vision coming to fruition upon you. Revelation calls to you in the star-filled nights of your sleep to the awakening of yourself as God. It is the beginning of your journey home.

The task is to bring forth the revelation of the stirrings of your soul, and insightful understanding to every level of your body, mind, and heart in all of your undertakings (thoughts, words, and actions) in three-dimensional characteristics, and beyond. The task at hand is to make yourself at one with these revealing experiences to the point where your consciousness is the allness of your experiences in completion and joyous freedom.

When your growing awareness in receptivity allows for this attunement, you shall continue forward in greater strides of expansion. But just as a baby in its youthful stage must have guidance, loving care, and constant attention, so, too, must your infant-like, revealing expansion be given the nurturing, care, and protection from those worldly energies or thoughts of limitation. Those energies shall attempt to interfere with your peace, and when you are unaware, they shall try to steal into your thoughts and disrupt your joy.

Just as with all inner experiences and altered states of expansion, each level is perceived through unique and different depths within self. Experiences of great and vast magnitude that move beyond revelation into a state of enlightenment, along with those quiet, inner promptings which allow you greater access to inner wisdom, have their place and moment of grace and allowance. All have their importance in the continuity of your path and purpose gained within your awareness. Each experience unto itself must be cultivated and processed within your being and awareness if succeeding experiences are to be received in greater abundance and understanding within self.

In other words, there is no end to your growing, expanded evolution in consciousness. In order to excel and progress without undue interruption and disruption, you should be aware of your infant stage of experience, and nurture your unfolding consciousness even as you would nurture your children.

This can be accomplished through chosen associations with friends with whom you surround yourself, making sure your unfolding consciousness is within a supportive, understanding, loving environment. This applies also through that which you consume in your mind and body, whether through foodstuffs or thought-forms. Be discriminating in what you consume. Television, books, and food are all taken upon your being on various levels of vibratory experience and either serve you or not, depending on their vibration. Be aware of your self and that which feels right to you. Then follow that design and plan for your highest good and unfoldment. The ease with which you flow with the river of yourself is dependent upon your own personal awareness, self-perception, and acceptance of your own truth. Seek not to change others but change yourself. Seek not to be anything other than that which you are: God in expression, God in awareness.

Superconsciousness, the permanent state of God-man realized, is that which awaits man in his Divine self and beckons to him now in these final days and years of transition upon Terra. It calls out to him through the revelation of Spirit-soul understanding and moves quickly upon him now as the increasing influx of higher energies infuses all of material Creation. The attainment of the superconsciousness state is that which we prepare you for and sustain within the ethereal realms to reflect back upon you your own increasing Light.

Within superconsciousness, one becomes aware of being the All in All, at one with the nowness, the Spirit of all being, and revels in the childlike simplicity of joyous union with all of life. When living and experiencing the fullness of dimensional awareness, man shall transcend the plane of duality, and function out of and within his own eternal, infinite nature in total trust and complete honesty. The superconscious realm of completion supersedes all other modes of thought and experience. It stands on its own as the final earthly acquisition to be attained. All that transpires after this Kingdom-of-Heaven consciousness is attained upon finer dimensions of evolvement or levels of being is quite beyond anything imaginable to present-day conception. The movement underway from revelation to superconsciousness progresses ever more rapidly now as those beings awakening to the Light within take hold of the power in which they reside and boldly step forth upon this dimensional frequency, speaking their truth, living their Love, and being their Light. All walks of life within all countries of this planet feel the ever-changing frequencies of Love coming upon them. Although they may be unaware of what, how, or why this is happening, they are perceiving their lives and love as more expansive and more forgiving each day.

The massive changes which are occurring in Europe and Russia are but the tip of the iceberg in relation to that which will come to the entire planet in days ahead. Although these alterations are seen, at the onset, to be painful and filled with hardship to those involved, what shall transpire and flow from these times shall truly be inspiring and obvious to all. They will see that it was necessary to have the experience, and that it was an essential process that had to occur for the greater revelation of union and Love to be fulfilled within the collective social consciousness.

All change requires a letting-go process in order for the greater purpose to be implemented. Those orders of limiting patterns of structured belief are difficult for many to relinquish. We see this upon a global scale. These beliefs must be dealt with, first and foremost, if the desired transformation is to be accomplished with greater ease. That is why we are here for you, to aid you in dispelling your fears and to free you from your own limiting thought-forms of old beliefs which bind you and restrict you from attaining the knowledge of yourself and your power.

As each being in the focus of unfoldment begins to receive experiences of revelation, he shall know within his heart of the greater plan of his life and move in choice that shall indeed lead him on his way to a superconscious state of being and enlightenment.

Blessed are all who desire oneness, and blessed are all who realize it is within themselves. May all come to perceive their God-self.

Om. Peace. Bliss. Understanding.

I am Jonathon.

XVIII

✦

Working with
Light Energies

✦

Becoming sensitively attuned to forces of accelerated Light frequency is highly important for all who are part of the Age of Love which comes swiftly into your dimension. There are many levels of sensitivity, from physical awareness on up to the higher spiritual and psychic attunement, available to those whose perceptual capabilities have been allowed to widen enough to focus upon swifter vibrational frequencies. All must be accessed on one level or another, depending on each given opportunity. The practice of working with Light energies, along with a basic knowledge of the forces and principles of Light and color, are desirable if you are to be a beacon guiding others to their deeper knowingness. The use of focused thought again comes into play in the process of unfolding energies of Light and the concentrated power therein to consciously direct energies for healing of the physical, mental, and emotional bodies, and for the purposes of sending or receiving thought images and information. All of this facilitates ascension of physical vibratory phenomena.

To begin with, all of Creation is, within its essence and structure of foundation, Light at various degrees of manifestation. All that you see and experience in your dimension is projected Light coalesced into matter frequencies, giving it the illusion of solidity, or structured phenomena. In its essence, it is Light, or Spirit energy, acting as animator of material Creation. There are a wide array of levels and sublevels of created structure. This holds true as well for those various Light frequencies which make up and design the uniform patterns of material Creation.

Your senses, although wondrous in their design, at present are unable to perceive the innumerable variations which make up the greater light spectrum of color, hue and vibrational beauty which infuse your world, body, and thoughts. All about you and within you, these Light energies dance to the melody of God's thought and are responsible for the platform of experience of the Earth and all contained therein. That which your senses perceive is but a fragment of all that truly is.

As consciousness expands and individual vibration exceeds the levels of past patterns, growth takes place upon all levels. The sensitivity of the individual in awareness of these Light frequencies becomes much more acute. In working with these energies of Light, we are directing your attention to elevated states of acceptance and the use of these Light frequencies to aid each individual consciousness to move to a state of greater self-awareness, healing, and planetary transformation for the greater good of All That Is.

Each individual entity enters this dimension upon a frequency band or particular ray, or upon a combination of rays of Light frequency. Throughout their incarnation, their birth ray directs and operates the course of their life on various levels. They are usually unconscious of this. The psychological, spiritual, emotional, and mental framework of each incarnating entity is influenced by their particular color or ray frequency. All choices are usually the reflection of this guiding force throughout their incarnation upon form. The bands of frequency change, however, as the individual's consciousness expands in Spirit, thus allowing greater choices and opportunities for individual progress to higher, more subtle frequencies of Light-ray influence and power.

Inner transformation is the alchemy of Light projection and manifestation within each evolving consciousness. The properties of Light are indeed endless and infinite because Light is God and you are that.

As the consciousness expands to the awareness that he, she, or it is God, and is Love and Light in manifestation, all things become possible because all Creation is open and available for utilization by the God-man Mind, at one with the Father Principle. Becoming aligned and attuned with the various Light frequencies is a natural side effect of evolving growth in awareness. There are practices to aid in the conscious alignment with these bands of Light which shall aid you in effecting change in physical, mental, emotional and spiritual bodies. These practices also promote health and well-being.

As the evolving consciousness is able to receive more Light, even greater change shall manifest, and life shall truly become a paradise upon Terra.

For now, let us begin with a few practices and discussions of various frequencies with which you are familiar in your perception of Light and color.

First, let me give you a brief explanation of that particular Light frequency which I and others of my fold work with and are upon. I am upon the seventh plane of Light manifestation which, in your understanding of color and frequency, would be considered violet in perception. In truth, your color perception cannot allow full appreciation or understanding of the immense beauty of the true band of frequency of the violet ray because it vibrates at such a highly distinct level upon the Creation of manifested Light that few upon Terra know or can experience it. Those who are able to truly perceive its awesome beauty are those who are advanced enough to withstand the vibratory acceleration of frequency which it transmits and radiates.

In my communication with you, I must decelerate certain bands of frequency in our alignment with you in order to accomplish clear connection and not cause harm to your body or mind. If I were to enter your consciousness in fullness upon the seventh ray of being, you could not withstand the extreme Light frequencies, and you would be harmed. Be not fearful, as I and those others of advanced wisdom and intelligence are fully aware of and in perfect understanding of the exact degree of manifest Light which can and cannot be revealed to you and all evolving consciousness. We would never put you or anyone in jeopardy physically, mentally, or emotionally. If we felt that someone could not handle the Light alterations and higher vibratory frequencies upon cellular or subcellular levels, we would not be in communication or alignment with their vibratory beingness. You are perfectly safe!

The seventh ray of frequency is by no means the highest of Light manifestation for there is no limit to God's Light and firmament therein. Yet, it indeed is a most powerful and magnificent frequency. Through it my body is able to traverse consciousness and access transformational properties of manifestation upon various levels of Creation. I find it most helpful and fascinating when utilizing its properties in dimensional understanding and travel. The seventh ray, or violet ray, is the frequency of transformation. That is why I and others of this ray are here now, to aid in this great task upon Terra. We utilize its wondrous qualities to effect transformation and transmutation of material and dimensional awareness to higher vibrational understanding. Upon this dimension, it has been the greatest transformational tool of Light alteration, and yet, there come to this schoolroom even greater, more powerful, more expanded Light energies. These are frequencies so profoundly magnificent as to bring the greatest minds of mastered Creation to their knees in humility.

This awesome Light of God's hierarchy and angelic might comes to reveal in their presence the waves of oceanic, cosmic transformation from within the heart of the One Light of All. We bow in humbleness of Spirit to these energies of frequency which, through their power, create worlds of wonder and awe. We look upon these vast energies of Love and grandness and, within the wonder of their presence, we proclaim, "Blessed be the Father Creator whose unlimited knowingness shows the way for all his children and brings them home to his doorstep!"

Now, each entity, as we spoke of earlier, carries within and around it the band of Light frequency which denotes its particular vibration and level of attainment in consciousness. As the entity expands in awareness, so does the band of Light vibration of which it is a part.

When working with Light energies, it is helpful to discern that particular frequency which is the primary band throughout the life incarnation if one is to be able to help oneself or others in their quest for greater health and spiritual unfoldment. In meditation one is able to acquire the primary frequency in open reception. As you sit in silence, focus on the third-eye area and project the desire to receive the primary band of individual vibration, and it shall come to you. The first color inwardly seen or perceived is usually the primary one. Colors perceived afterward are usually secondary life-wave bands which are influential but are not as potent or as powerful as the primary one.

For instance, if within the meditative state the color yellow is perceived as a primary band, this implies that the yellow ray of life Creation is influencing your life and direction. This would imply that the individual is mentally and creatively oriented, functioning for the most part upon higher thought and yet is still very much a part of material manifestation. Yellow band rays are those who operate with a great deal of mental agility and spiritual wisdom unfolding in their lives. They are usually mature or older souls who are very close to illumination or deeper realization. Their task is to exceed the band on which they entered this plane and incorporate other frequencies of various character into their auric field and subtle bodies. This is to bring them into alignment with more advanced frequencies of gold-pink or violet. As they break down the barriers of these vibratory frequencies through greater openings, they incorporate those frequencies into their beingness and attain greater leaps in unfolding awareness and states of self-mastery.

Throughout the expansion of self-evolving awareness, these Light frequencies shall become more apparent as your consciousness opens to the degree of perception of their validity and impact upon your reality. As the evolving entity receives the subtle impressions of vibratory Light and color in greater intensity and degree, it shall be able to differentiate and utilize those particular frequencies of color and vibration which shall be most appropriately applied to increase vibrational unfoldment, improve health, and manifest those changes within awareness that shall aid in any number of levels, physical or spiritual.

Just as certain frequencies of sound and melody produce transformation in consciousness within emotional and psychological bodies, so, too, does the use of Light and color vibrations produce peace-filled and expanded states when properly used and directed toward upliftment. Certain colors in one's environment produce various moods, or states of emotional vibration, and can be either an aid or a hindrance to energies of awakening and joyous mind states. For instance, if one's primary lifestream color were red, we would suggest the use of light and deep blues to facilitate a greater alignment. The balance of light and color energies within the individual is significant in producing and promoting healthier states. If one's primary color were red, and if he or she could infuse their living quarters or other surroundings with those hues of blue or green, he would greatly benefit.

Utilizing the color spectrum in one's living space is but one simple way of aiding oneself in alignment and balance. Visualization of those desired color frequencies during meditative states is yet another method and practice of working with the light energies. As alignment and balance are restored in the various bodies, a greater, more expanded state of consciousness shall ensue, and the entity shall evolve at even greater acceleration to higher awareness states. The use of light and color, when combined and enhanced through sound vibration and melody, can also produce powerful and extraordinary transformation.

Bringing the various bodies into alignment is the goal of light-energy usage. Through that alignment, the consciousness is freed to evolve with less of the dense energies and thought-forms which prevent the awareness from perceiving finer realms of being.

XIX

✦

*The Death
Transition*

✦

D eath, and the fear surrounding this transition, has been a most profound yet misunderstood phenomenon for many who are terrified of the prospect of after-death states or the end of existence at death transition. Many live their lives in the haunting terror which virtually immobilizes them in their choices and potential joy of life.

Within the social drama, we view the mass consciousness still plagued by those fears, doubts, and uncertainty of the validity or reality of there being an evolving, after-death state in which their identity and consciousness would be preserved and kept secure. There is, however, the beginning of a shift in awareness with regard to this. Part of our intention in this communication process is to assure you that indeed your consciousness and identity are ever evolving, safe, and beyond the transition termed death. You shall indeed survive, and quite well, I might add, after the moment of departure from your physical shell at the completion of your lessons in the dream upon Terra.

At the moment when your physical life energies begin to wane and decline, you shall feel a shift of awareness, a surge of energy that shall propel you out of your encasement into a higher vibrational dimension of Spirit essence, outside the physical vibrational field. Your awareness and conscious identity shall be acute and greatly enhanced as you are confronted by those beings with whom you have connection, either in past-life interaction or multidimensional experiences, or by those entities or guides of higher frequency that are in service to you. Your joy shall be great as the physical shell is dropped and your freedom of expansion supersedes all past pain, struggle, or misfortune which you experienced on the physical plane. You shall be shown the entirety of your physical life just experienced in form, including all thoughts, actions, words, deeds, desires, joys, sorrows, gains, and losses, and be given spiritual understanding of the lessons learned therein.

Each entity within form exists within the reality of his own truth and level of evolvement. Upon the exit of form, each carries with him those beliefs, thoughts, and fears of all that made up the totality of self-identity and consciousness. Those rigidly held beliefs of a particular after-life state shall be met and enacted upon at the time of the release from the physical state because all thoughts and beliefs create reality. However, there are those higher entities who shall be present to inform the newly transitioned entity of the true nature and character of his state and the illusory nature of his beliefs or fears. They shall guide him to the vibrational level of evolving placement within Spirit Essence. There are those souls who deny, through willfulness, the greater understanding and hold fast to those beliefs or fears which limit their evolving consciousness. They ignore and do not hear their higher guidance and become stuck in the apparitional character of their own thought-fear Creation. This usually does not continue for long, however, for the entity begins to tire of the endlessness of this immobile state and longs for greater Light and understanding. He thus receives immediate attention and clarification of his true predicament and security within God's Spirit.

The entity then moves to that placement of soul vibration which is in likeness with his own, and receives instruction through different spiritual lessons and experiences as to his highest purpose and development in areas of greatest growth, whether in dimensional, formless being, or upon the many other physical dimensions of expression within universal Creation. Depending on the soul's development, he is guided by higher beings to choose those paths which will accelerate the learning process and allow him to experience those lessons which will give him the highest possible joy, oneness, and wisdom in connection with his ultimate union with Spirit-Light knowingness.

If the soul has much to learn and experience and is guided to choose to incarnate in physical expression in order to widen the gates of wisdom within, he shall incarnate in the area, to the parents, and in the circumstances chosen by his higher self and Spirit guidance which, hopefully, will enable him to accomplish his mission and learn his lessons. As with all things, free will is always in effect. It is up to the individual as to whether or not those lessons are seen and accepted upon the incarnation. All must be learned according to the individual's truth within if one is to evolve and graduate to higher states of awareness. These lessons, although completely unique to each evolving being, have behind and within them the structure of universal harmony and laws that must be seen and understood if the entity is to progress to greater Light. The universal Law of Love is the only true lesson. Wisdom of that is to be gained and understood because, through its unfoldment within the individual consciousness, the mastery of physical expression and formless dimensional experience is attained, thereby freeing the soul to move out of physical incarnation and into greater expression and evolvement within God's unlimited kingdoms.

As the soul achieves illumination within form of his union with the God of his being, he then moves on to higher and higher levels of attainment and spiritual power quite beyond anything imaginable to third-dimensional perspectives, yet evolving ever onward, ever inward in harmony, Light and unlimited Love.

Fear of death is a pattern of thought which has been programmed into your soul over many incarnations. It must be released in the Light of understanding. You must realize that your being is eternal, birthless, and deathless. You are temporarily within this drama of physical expression to learn and evolve, and yet your home, your true place, is within your God-self, within your spiritual kingdom. Your safety and infinite being are secure now and always, no matter what happens in the drama of physical life, no matter what harm or misfortune befalls your body form. You are not your body or mind. You are the spark of Light of your Father Creator and are all-powerful, all-wise within your highest being-self. Therefore, your self-created thought forms of the fear of death transition must be seen, understood, and then finally released because they do not serve you in your greater knowing.

Death is an illusion among your fearful concepts. It is indeed a safe and pleasant experience for it frees you from your bondage within Earth's experience. It allows you to move on to greater levels of joyous expansion.

Death is but a breath of change, a moment of upliftment to a freer state, a heartbeat of heavenly emancipation from the struggles, travails, and heartbreaks of the density of matter and pain therein. Be not fearful, therefore, of that which is your good and trusted friend and ally in your liberation from matter. Be more concerned with the nows in your present life and the present moment. Focus on the acquisition of your spiritual heritage in union with God so that when the angel of death comes calling upon you, you shall be ready and willing to fly with wings of joy. Understand that your soul is forever free in God, forever safe, forever loved!

XX

✦

*The Illusion of
Time and Space*

✦

Within the fabric of molecular, three-dimensional density, the structure and formation of the illusion of time and space reside. The concept is that, in reality, there is form and subsequent space surrounding that form and its equivalent, time, which is the concept and perception of past, present, and future. This leads the human consciousness to believe in beginnings and endings, birth and death. We are here to dispute this misunderstanding and, hopefully, clarify the truth of the matter which, when fully perceived through a grander overview of alignment with Spirit understanding, shall lead to the deeper knowing that space and time are meaningless. Within your current understanding, your senses relate to you the perception that time and space are real. Let us take a closer look.

The Illusion of Time

The illusion termed "time" in your reality does indeed exist because it is part of the mass social incarnating agreement as to its validity and reality within the system of belief structure. In other words, because the concept of time – the perceived beginnings and endings, change of seasons, and youth to old age, for example – is rigidly held and agreed upon by the human consciousness, the greater reality of

timelessness and interaction with multilevels of multidimensional existence occurring simultaneously remains unseen and unknown by most of
Humanity. Locked within the limited structure of yesterday, today, and
tomorrow, the human consciousness fails to perceive the eternal nowness of being which is ever present and ever unfolding and which
encompasses the infinite winds of all experience. The fact that the
conscious thought of all or most of Humanity is in agreement with this
concept makes the accessibility and availability of greater avenues of
unlimited experience within the timeless aspects of their being more
difficult. Belief-created reality is your truth and experience, and what
you believe shall indeed be. But the structure of belief is limiting to an
unlimited being, and in your God-knowing self, you are indeed unlimited. The day of awakening has come, and the shackles of beliefs
which do not serve you must be undone and discarded if you are to move
forward in understanding of your true nature.

Time and the concept of past-present-future is, when properly
viewed, merely that — a concept and nothing more. All experience, all
life within all dimensions of being are moving within the nowness of
God's thought, and that Infinite Mind of which you are a part is timeless
and without space. The concept of infinity, or timelessness, is beyond
human, third-dimensional perception using the five senses, and it must
again be experienced through those finer perceptions of self within
higher-self states. The validity of this timeless understanding will never
be seen or perceived by man in his present state for it goes against all
that seems reasonable and within this belief structure, which limits his
higher perceptual capabilities. Man must go within to his God-self
connection to begin to view that quality of timeless, infinite experience
which is, was, and always shall be his own. For the God-Force Principle,
being eternal, infinite thought-consciousness and all projections of his
beingness, experiences all in the moment, in the nowness of eternity, all
experience, all life, all complete within the perfection of his being. Now
is eternal, infinite, timeless being, and you are that.

Within your timeless being, which knows no birth or death and no
beginnings or endings, you are experiencing all of your lives within form
and in formlessness within that God-Force-Principle Spirit in the forever-

ness of your being. At this very moment, the simultaneity of your experience within your own multidimensional self is contained in completeness of thought within the mind of God. As you connect to that Spirit of truth within you, you shall indeed perceive the timelessness of your self and the multilevels of experience of which you are a part. In that revelation, you shall perceive that indeed there are no boundaries to yourself, no limitations to past-present-future orientation, and you shall know the freedom and joy of now.

If you will take a moment to reflect upon your early life and recall when it was that you seemed to experience time, you will remember that "then" was the "now" within your mind and understanding; and just as yesterday seems but a dream of the past, it indeed is just as much now as your tomorrow will be and is this moment. There is only one place where your experience, revelation, and true perception can be and that is now, within the timeless expanse of your being, which is God. This is truly the path to your self, for when all of your perceptions, experiences, and one-pointed awareness are held to your nowness of being, you shall know your God. For your God, your true self, is in the timeless, joyous now of its being and awaits your awakening to now, and your own union therein.

When, upon the transition of death, your awareness is greatly increased, you shall converge and converse with those beings who shall aid you and reveal to you in the timelessness of your experience within form every thought, word, and deed which was part of your experience. You shall experience a taste of your own foreverness. As your consciousness expands to perceive greater levels of multidimensional understanding, you shall perceive to a much greater degree the true character of your Spirit.

This understanding does not have to come at that transitional point called death, however, because the capability of experiencing the timeless characteristics of your nature is upon you now as we communicate with you. Upon the moment of this now, within your being, you are connecting in awareness with the greater alignment of Spirit and Eternal, Infinite Mind.

When you are in the complete and total awareness of the nowness of your being in concentrated joy, and of your play in the drama of Creation, you are truly yourself. Your joy knows no boundaries, no limits or structures therein. Life then becomes boundless, infinite bliss within the timelessness and the nowness of your own God-self.

The Illusion of Space

Within third-dimensional form, matter is perceived as solid and containing properties and aspects of structure which allude to the concept of space and matter. Yet this is known as being untrue, even when perceived with high-powered technology devised by man himself. Matter is condensed form and vibration held intact by the higher God-Force Principle. It is simply coalesced and condensed thought. The atomic, vibratory density of form interacts with multilevels of Creation, and Spirit flows within and around each particle and each molecule, thereby producing the movement, the life within each cell and atom. The lifetrons, or minute particles of God's thought, activate each atomic and molecular structure to carry forth those messages of Love which hold that thought or form within characteristic structure. Yet, there is no true, solid form or matter because all is thought, agreed upon and brought together for the agreement of experience within form.

Upon the third-dimensional experience, your five perceptions formulate these concepts for use and function upon your density of matter and experience of living therein. Your senses are devised as tools for your soul's use in matter, and yet, their reliance has been, for the most part a deterrent when seeking inward a greater perceptual capability. When the senses, through stillness, are shut down and ignored for certain periods of time, as in meditative states, other finer, inner sensitivities are awakened, leading to more advanced and evolved perceptions of the true inner reality. This is yet another reason for disciplining your time and life to allow for meditative practice because your own awakening power and inner senses shall come to you and reveal to your own mind and life that which is real and true.

Now, within the many multidimensional frequencies existing about and within you, these overlap and parallel your now. They are in touch with your oversoul at all times, in connection and communication with all your thoughts and experiences. There are countless multidimensional levels alive and in motion right upon the place you find yourself at this moment. If your inner senses were awakened from dormancy, you would be capable of perceiving them in their fullness and subtlety of character and interact through conscious communion. This would be accomplished in two ways: either by the use of the created omnidimensional body, whereby your body vibration could be dematerialized and reformed upon the particular dimensional vibration or character of that individual plane, enabling you to communicate and share in the interaction; or simply by inwardly attuning to those inner sensitivities and opening up those subtle avenues of reception to those particular vibrational dimensions, as in the communication with that of my being at this moment.

When perceived in this manner, the rigid structure of matter becomes illusory and is seen as that which it truly is — yet another vibratory dimensional frequency which can be transcended and manipulated in relation to the soul's purpose and intention in Light. Form was never meant to restrict but rather to instruct the soul within to the ultimate awareness of its boundless power and capability. Instead, through the eons of dense experiences, it became the prison of flesh for the unawakened soul, trapped in the cycle of rebirth. Through lifetime after lifetime of physical incarnational experiences, the soul, although formless, omnipresent Spirit, believed and conceived itself to be separate from the greater, whole God-Force Principle and thus gathered yet heavier, more powerful chains about it, forging an even more restrictive prison cell from which it would eventually have to break free through self-realized liberation.

Time and space, therefore, when perceived from a lofty view outside of structured matter, is ever-changing, inconstant, and dreamlike because, in its unstable character, it can be reshaped within consciousness and dimensional experience. When time is altered in your inner experience through expanded consciousness states such as meditation or intense concentration in work or play, the character of your individual experience and your conception or perception of those moments is reformed and shaped by your own consciousness, manipulated by you.

When your love is upon the action of something such as your concept of time, moments within time become meaningless, for you are in the nowness of oneness with yourself, and your experience becomes timeless.

As I view your history and perceive your various multifaceted, multidimensional experiences, I am able to see your past, present, and future incarnations as existing in the nowness of being. It is not merely that I am presently out of physical, third-dimensional properties but that, within my consciousness, I am fully capable of adjusting my vibratory field of receptivity to account for the various vibrational structures. I can align my being with the boundless aspects of you to view your totality in the ever-moving, ever-changing now. This is your destiny, and that of all mankind as well, as you awaken to higher principles of formless identity and vibrational understanding. The universal structure of the cosmic plan of unfoldment and cycles of evolution therein now bring to man this opportunity and information for his awakening. Reflect upon this well and perceive its truth within you.

XXI ✦

Questions and Answers

✦

Question to Jonathon: What was your last incarnation upon Earth, and when and where was it?

It was upon the continent of Europe, in eastern France, that I spent my last incarnation within form. My name was also Jonathon in that particular expression. I have kept it as part of the totality of my past and present vibration. I lived approximately during the years A.D. 1250-1300 in Earth times, and within that era and life span, my subsequent illumination took place. My life was dedicated at an early age to the acquisition of higher understanding, and although I worshipped within the restrictions of structured Christianity, I came to realize my place within the universal Heart of the Father within.

I became a monk in an early order of fellow brothers who, living the life of discipline and self-denial, spent most of their days in duties devoted to meditative and prayerful endeavors. Other time was allocated to serving those who came to us for spiritual aid and for help with general physical ills. Our order was relatively small and consisted of several souls of great intuitive insight and spiritual understanding. By your standards of living, it would be seen as a most boring, uneventful period and yet, that which took place within my soul was my mastery of self and the ending of all physical desires which led to that wondrous moment of revelation when the heavens parted and the darkness of my soul was no more!

It was a very simple life indeed. We ate little, slept little, and directed our energies to the pursuit of the ways of our master, Jesus. We slept on hard floors, spoke little to each other, had periods of fasting, and spent many, many hours in silent, inward preoccupation with the Lord of our hearts. It was a life of Spirit, a hard life at times, yet one that I loved and chose for the fulfillment of my days and nights in close communion with God. Our order was poor and relied upon the support, faith, and generosity of the townspeople for our survival needs. We did, however, have a small garden by the side of our sleeping quarters. I dearly loved it and spent many happy hours working, digging, and planting the seeds that germinated and grew to fruition.

Ah, the joy of that simple setting fills me even now as I speak of it! My great joy was in watching the wonder of Creation as the seed grew to fullness and the vegetables found their way into the Divine hands of those who used them for food. The miracle of life was all around me then, and I drank of the nectar of God's Love daily.

Our abbey was quite small and consisted of one building which was the living quarters, and two smaller, stone huts which were used for various purposes such as storage as well as meditation cells, where we could retreat when we chose, or were directed to remain alone in silent contemplation. Two of our brothers spent a great deal of time in silent retreat within those walls at the direction of their own inner guidance, spending weeks at a time in total isolation.

Those of us who were assigned the task of their well-being would silently take food to the cell door and place it under an opening at the bottom, being careful not to make a sound which might disturb their peace and solitude.

When the planting of the garden was good and the season plentiful, we would gather our harvest and distribute food among the needy townspeople and those whose hunger was greater than our own. Many harvests were good; others were not. Several of us were given the responsibility of cooking, cleaning, and general maintenance of the quarters. All work was done in silent, joyful reverence.

I, myself, was one who was assigned a variety of duties, and at times, I would steal away after their completion and take long walks in the woods and surrounding hills. How I loved those walks alone, the smell of the trees and tall grass blowing in the wind, the sound of the fallen leaves in autumn as they crackled underfoot, the wonder-filled sights of the children laughing and playing by the edge of the river. My heart becomes overwhelmed when I think of the vast beauty of this dimension and the joy that is found therein. Even now, I soar to that place and revel in those moments.

It was there, by a stream, that I saw my Lord. It was a beautiful spring day. The sun was warm and the birds were singing their songs of love. It was a most perfect day, indeed. I was out alone on one of my walks, contemplating my life and the issues I was dealing with which concerned one of the brothers of my order. The path I was on went down to a stream, and as I got nearer to it, I heard my name spoken softly. I turned but saw nothing. Pausing silently for a brief moment, I then turned back toward the stream and path. There, standing before me, was my Lord Jesus, his hands outstretched, and an expression on his face which filled my being with such awe and joy that I knew it was he.

The Light was so bright, and it extended out in all directions from his body form. I was overwhelmed by his power and Love as he spoke gently:

"Brother Jonathon, thou hast been called upon to apply thyself to my Word, my Love, and that of my Father within. Thou shalt lift up the sheep in my Father's flock and carry them across the stream of life's worldly woes and deliver them to my Father's Kingdom. I shall guide thee and be with thee, always."

And with those words, he smiled an angelic smile so filled with Love that I dropped to my knees as my power to stand left me. As I looked up, he was gone, vanishing before my sight, and all that lingered was profound silence and stillness of nature all around me as if in reverence to "He who cometh in the night to proclaim the dawning of a new day."

My senses were overcome by the experience, and as I sat and prayed in that Divine moment, blessing the Father for His Love and expression, there dawned upon my closed eyes a great golden-white Light that filled my inner gaze. The Hand of God touched my soul, lifting it up into blissful, loving awareness of Spirit's oneness with myself and all of Creation.

The consciousness of the cosmos was upon me and I swooned in the ecstasy of peace and union. I then knew of life's true purpose, of my part within the order of things. Divine Truth and Light became one with my being. I viewed past, present, and future as being part of the same moment. The fiery expansion of the birth of Creation fell before my humbled gaze. I was in this state for but a moment, and yet, eternity lay before me within that single breath of time.

As I returned to the abbey, the others gathered around me, seeing my changed expression. I could not speak. I could not utter a sound for the experience was of such magnitude within my soul that words seemed meaningless and futile. I retreated to my isolation for approximately three weeks before conferring with my brothers about that which had blessed my being that day by the stream.

As I speak of this day, I again become that experience and blend with the utterly incomprehensible beauty and Love I felt. I praise the Lord God of my being for the blessing that allowed me the breaking of those chains which bound me to earthly form. Although this Earth is filled with beauty of great wonder, the beauty which filled my soul to overflowing revealed to me the joy to be found within the higher frequencies of Spirit-consciousness.

Revelation can come at any moment — as you walk by a stream, sit upon your bed, or even as your eyes look out upon a star-filled night. The Lord God of your being may come and take you by the hand and lead you to your destiny. Be prepared through stillness of thought, for that which is to come shall provide the key to your freedom from the prison of past beliefs. Once you are given this peace and awareness, your wings shall outstretch and your Spirit shall soar on the winds of timelessness to the Kingdom of God within!

How old were you when you had this vision and spiritual experience?

It was in the springtime of my forty-sixth year in service to our Lord. In all honesty, dear brother, I must say that it truly was much more, much greater than that of a mere vision. In its wake, my entire life was altered and transformed and the expansion of consciousness superseded all other forms of normalcy of thought. Through the experience, my being was uplifted and changed in all ways and on all levels. Previous to the experience, my life was lived within the confines of faith, trust, and belief in the order of Divine Law as set down by our Lord, Jesus Christ. All of my devotions and work were carried out with the secret hope of one day truly knowing that which I so fervently believed, according to my faith. And yet, when that sublime experience occurred, it banished forever the concepts, beliefs, and structured walls of limited awareness which I had previously known and by which I had lived my entire life.

Before the experience, I was prone to more serious views. Afterward, I was able to laugh and play in the innocence of a child seeing the world for the first time. The experience altered my perception of myself as being mortal. I was no longer plagued with fearful thoughts of tortured souls paying penance to a fearful God. I viewed myself in entirety as the Allness, the Love, and the everlasting Spirit of kindness, laughter, and mirth.

My soul, heart, and mind became one with the God of my being and the whole world and the entire universe transformed before me. I was no longer a mere man of God for I realized I was God as all are, although they know it not.

How old were you when you died and how did you die?

It was an especially bitter winter during my forty-ninth year in physical form when the angel of death lifted me upon his wings of flight. We were visited by torrents of freezing rain and storms with bitterly cold winds that left many of us ill. I was one of several who were suffering with the consumption of the breakdown of vital organs connected with breathing. My illness became more serious as the cold months continued, and I labored in ill health, attempting to care for the others who, at the time, were faring worse than I. Several brothers gave up their bodies, and I was the last to give up mine.

Exhausted and drained by the long hours of wakefulness in an attempt to prolong the lives of those few who I felt were depending on me, I collapsed. As I lay in death's wing, my brothers stood before me, praying and weeping, and I began to see the room fill with Light before my eyes. I realized the moment had come to vanquish the shell I had grown so accustomed to during those forty-nine years. I left my body easily and painlessly and was met by my master, Jesus, who lovingly guided me to heavenly fields of Light and laughter.

What was the name of the monastic order to which you belonged?

It was a small order which was part of a much larger one known to be spread out through central Europe. The larger order was termed the Order of the Brothers of the Holy Cross. We simply went by the title of The Brothers for those whom we served and who knew us. Our order was small, amounting to not more than twenty-five at any given time.

Death was a normal part of our lives as the life span was not as great as it is in this time. My age at transition was considered quite old to many who, at that time, did not live past thirty years. The usual number of brothers was between fifteen and eighteen as time brought forth and then took away those of our order.

After your spiritual revelation, did you experience any supernatural powers or abilities previously unknown to you?

Yes, there were those who experienced healing though my touch. Psychic doorways were flung wide open, affording me the ability to see that which was yet to be. After the initial awakening, I experienced greater sensitivity to the inner realms as well as to outer physical sensory perception. I found it quite easy to exit the body in order to traverse wide distances, appearing before other brothers and viewing distant experiences. I would fall into moments of ecstasy when the oneness of Spirit would overtake me, filling me with its joy. Many other abilities also followed my awakening into Light.

Why did you have to die? Why did you not just ascend and create an

omnidimensional body for yourself?

Dear brother, you must understand that at the time of my awakening in that era, knowledge of this depth was kept hidden except to those chosen initiates of secret orders who, through the aid of mastermind sages, or adepts, were able to gain the knowledge whereby they could become skilled in this. You must also understand that at that period, the energies of vibratory frequency were much denser than they are now, and the opportunity of being a part of this knowledge was far less than it is now. At the time, my focus was not placed on securing a dimensional means of travel for I was established in the knowingness and Love of my eternal Spirit nature. The application and formation of the omnidimensional body came after my physical departure.

I have learned much and evolved a great deal since that incarnation. I have acquired those skills which afford me that which was previously unknown. We are all learning and are part of the evolution of beingness, brother, and yes, I, too, have much to learn. Just because I, at this time, have certain knowledge and usage of it does not preclude the fact that all of Creation is within the spiral of upward mobility back to the heart of God. It does not preclude my ceasing to evolve.

All is in motion within God's dream. There are those advanced beings of the Celestial Hierarchy who are so highly evolved that they make my being appear to be as a small child before them. There is no end to the Infinite Mind of God and his Creation. Spirit is in constant motion, and knowledge is given to and acquired by only those who are ready to receive it and hold the responsibility that comes with that knowledge.

There is no judgment for those at lesser levels of evolvement for the Great Spirit-Infinite Mind understands that all are evolving at their own paces and all are doing the best they can, given their experiences in form and out of form.

It was my choice to leave the final encasement of my last earthly incarnation behind for it was aged and worn out, like old clothes that have outlived their use. Within the freedom of the after-state, I found that all is truly possible through focused desire and higher dimensional thought. That freedom has allowed my being to experience great joy and endless Love.

Within the timelessness of God's thought, I have traveled extensively in countless dimensions of being and have been part of the Creation of worlds and life forms therein. I have learned the oneness of Spirit and experienced its power and might within the smallest of physical atoms and within the largest of planetary and interdimensional bodies. Truly, there is no end to this infinite cosmos of which we are all a part, nor could there ever be, for within the mind of God, all rests safe and secure and is in process of expansion at all levels of reality.

In your final incarnation, did you have any further experiences of cosmic consciousness after your initial experience?

Yes, my brother, after my initial experience of revelation, which completely altered my consciousness, I experienced other, even more profound periods of expanded awareness to the point where, in my final year of physical life, I was able to control the blissful experience of God-awareness. The energies were alive and moving within my being, and all that was necessary was for my thoughts to turn toward my Father in Love and connection, and my heart, mind, and soul would soar in the heavens of blissful awareness.

At times, it became a nuisance to those brothers who, upon finding me lost within trances, had to watch over me lest I might fall down or hurt myself unknowingly. It was not that I became irresponsible or unable to take care of myself, but when the Spirit of Infinite Love and Light came upon me and lifted my consciousness heavenward, all worldly, earthly cares or thoughts of physical reality left me, and my God-self carried me away to higher and higher states of bliss. There were moments within that bliss of unearthly awareness when I was seen floating and hovering above the garden or storage houses. I was lifted skyward by the Lightness of my being within my joy of God. Since it was not a phenomenon of great popularity or a skill easily acquired, my brothers stood about in awe. As it became increasingly evident that my heavenly state of mind was, at these times, spontaneously at fault for these acts of flight, they came to view it as, "Oh, there goes Brother

Jonathon again, taking to the air as if he were a bird and in a natural state for the brother whose head and body is in the clouds." It was a rather humorous event at times, and one in which I was thoroughly and blissfully unaware.

As my physical body became increasingly used to these high vibrations within me, the cellular rate and vibratory frequency of the matter of my body increased to such an extent that gravity became meaningless. As the weight of matter which made up the physical aspect of my being became aligned with the Spirit of higher, faster vibrations, I was rendered weightless. This, as I later came to learn, was not an uncommon phenomenon for one whose consciousness was aligned with Spirit. It became a rather unnerving experience at times, especially when it happened unexpectedly.

How does one know that it is one's last lifetime on this planet and wheel of rebirth?

One may know it is his last incarnation upon physical density when he has fully and completely realized his oneness with the God of his being. The initial spiritual connection is enough at times. At other times, it is not, for the consciousness must become at one with the higher frequencies and know beyond a doubt of its divinity within matter. Through that knowingness, in union, one must make the final decision as to the cessation of birth into form. There are those like me who choose not to incarnate again but prefer to work in Spirit-essence energies to aid the planet and Humanity. There are those other brothers and Light beings of great awakening who choose, through their own Divine desire, to serve Humanity as guides or teachers through incarnating into third-dimensional existence.

Many master souls are now upon this mission and are being born to aid in the awakening and transformation of Terra. Do not be surprised by the advent of wondrously wise entities of Light seen within the smiles and eyes of babes and young children.

"And a child shall lead them," is indeed a statement of prophetic truth found within your Bible, and one which will astound and confound a great many of your race. Yet it shall be so, and you shall bear witness to this.

The final decision not to incarnate again always rests with the God of your being. The complete union of your soul with God-spirit will reveal to you the necessity or non-necessity to continue upon the chains of rebirth into the physical. Your guides and master teachers who have been with you always in their evolvement and work with your being will be freed as well to move on to greater service as you move past the need for physical lessons. They, in their Love, patience, and devotion to your being, rejoice in your graduation from Earth school, and in their level of reality and vibration, graduate as well. They are then promoted to higher levels of responsibility within God's mansion and kingdoms.

The wondrousness of Infinity is truly beyond words, and the joy found in expanded levels becomes greater as the soul evolves higher and higher, experiencing yet more subtleties of vibration and unconditional Love and Light. There is no end to the evolution of soul and Spirit for all is in motion, and the cycle of God's thought is truly endless.

So what you are saying is that there is never an end in all of eternity, and that we continue on and on and become more and more evolved through many levels of experience. What is the ultimate purpose of it all?

Yes, that is correct. The ultimate purpose of gaining experience through Earth lifetimes and expanding experience in other finer dimensions of consciousness is to add to the ever-evolving fullness of the Mind of God. As your evolution grows, and you become lighter and filled with greater awareness of your God-self, it does not end there. The infinite, boundless Mind of God which supports and sustains you and of which you are a part is ever in the expansion of itself through your experiences and unfoldment. Truly, you are a valuable, necessary part of the wholeness of God's thought because your part and function adds to the whole. As your unfoldment increases, so does the Infinite Father-God Principle in its totality.

Are you saying that if I were not here, neither would God be here?

Correct. Every thought within the Infinite Mind of the Creator is invaluable and precious. This is confirmation of its infinite place within the cosmos as well. It can never not be. That which is shall always be within the blissful heart of the Father and within His Love. Therefore, you are worthy of your Love because your Spirit God-self, in endless continuance, now and forever, shall always be continually evolving, transforming, and ascending to greater heights of Light and Love with the mind of the Father Principle. Do you understand?

I think so. It is just so hard to conceive of an endlessness to things; yet, when I stop to consider, it is really difficult to imagine myself coming to an end.

Exactly! Within your deepest knowingness, you have feelings of your own impossible ending and "nothingness." For you to become a non-thought within the loving mind of God would be as impossible as the Mind of God becoming a "no thing." All are equal in the eyes of God. Since all things are equal, they have an equal part to play in the act of thought. The Infinite Mind holds all thoughts dear and loved as He is all thought and all thoughts are He.

So you and I are merely thoughts?

Yes, my brother, you and I are thoughts within the loving mind of the Father Principle, but not just thoughts, for we are divinely connected to the Spirit of All That Is. Being one with the wholeness of God's being, we are kinship to all the Father is, was, and evermore shall be. Not "mere thoughts," my learning brother, but Divine, blessed, omnipresent, infinite, joyous, loving, Lightbeing thoughts held within the Father's heart. All that the Father is, we are; and all that we are, the Father is. The more we evolve and become, the greater the Father becomes.

As I look out upon the world, it is hard for me to imagine this world changing or being lost without me in it.

Oh, but it would be, my friend, for all things are connected to your being because your being is God in expression and experience. Through your connection with All That Is, your part in the drama of third-dimensional experience is invaluable and necessary, especially at this time of the awakening of Terra and the Light energies coming forth. Your being shall always be, but your presence upon this form shall prove to be a Light to others who seek their way in the darkness. If it were that I and those of my group deemed you unworthy of the task at hand, and that your being was of no use for our purposes and the purposes of Him whom we serve, we would not be communicating with you now. Revere yourself, Love yourself, know your worth. See yourself as you are: a Divine spark of God-mind, ever new, alive and expanding into fullness of Light and Love. Be God, even as God is you. Realize your part. Your place is secure within the ever loving, all-knowing thought of God. Rejoice in the play of Creation; laugh at the ever-changing acts in the game of life. Smile in the knowingness that you and I are forever and have no end but own the never-failing Light of God's unending Love.

I suppose that it is my ego or personal self that has some difficulty with the idea of being a thought, and yet it does seem to register within me as making sense.

It is only your limited concept and finite perception of intellect that prevent you from seeing the fullness of that which I am speaking. You must understand that your mind, which is used to five-sense experience, is not used to the concept of Infinite Thought. When you think a thought upon your consciousness, you are witness to its beginning and end, coming and going within your mind. You are not in the understanding of the greater thought-creation of your Father who, within His infinite, loving mind sustains you and holds you in the perfection and endlessness of your being.

Within your human, limited consciousness, you witness imperfection, beginnings and endings. You fail to perceive that which, when viewed on a limited scale, is impossible to know. Yet, when viewed from the loftiness of God-mind awakened within you, one with your Father Principle, you may not only perceive that which you are within the mind of God, but you may be as the Father is, and within that awesome power, create, using the mind stuff of universal God-mind, all that you wish and desire through perfected thought. In your God-state, all is indeed possible and is given to you because your connection is one. You are no longer a mere wave but have the might and power of the ocean of God behind you and within you to bring forth all that is within your God-mind.

The great master Jesus revealed this basic truth to mankind when he, through his connection and oneness with the Father-Spirit Principle, was able to heal the sick, walk on water, disappear and reappear at will, and perform countless other acts of seeming incredibility, all being natural functions of the God-man.

When man, through his alignment with the God of his being, is able to perceive true creative thought and hold it within focus of desire and will, he, too, shall be able to accomplish easily the natural phenomena of God-man mind and shall reveal the kingdom of Love that God has had in store for his evolutionary children all along.

Thoughts are things, and in your mind they have their power to manifest when strongly felt and desired. If, at this moment, you were at one with your God-self in consciousness and full awareness, your thoughts would have the power and might of the Father-Principle behind them. You would see their instant creation into physical dimension beingness. This is the destiny of all who follow the will of Spirit and evolve into their God-self connection. Know that through and with this all-knowing force, you shall be able to command the winds, and they shall cease. Command to the elements, and they shall do your bidding. Speak the word, and those who suffer disease shall be made whole.

This, my brother, is that which shall be forthcoming to the God-man of this New Age of Coming Light.

You shall witness events of such extraordinary proportion so as to render your present mind into a state of total awe, and yet, these events shall be the natural unfoldment of God-consciousness and the birthright of the Son when at one with the Father.

In your days and nights of thought, my brother, always be in the desire of "thy will, not mine, be done and followed, my Infinite Loving Father." Keep His Love in your heart, and know deeply within your being that you are Divine because your being is one with your Father, and therefore is birthless, deathless, endless joy, bliss, and peace.

Walk in the Light of your Divine nature and all shall be well with you.
Om. Peace. Bliss. Understanding.
I am Jonathon, Speaker of the Council of the Brotherhood of Light.

**You spoke of the new God-man's expanding into culmination of
final mastery of material Creation. Could you clarify this? I
thought that the expansion of consciousness was unlimited, yet you
speak of a culmination.**

The expansion of consciousness knows no limits and is an endlessly
evolving phenomenon. The culmination spoken of refers to the material
plane of manifestation and the complete and total understanding and
use of powers available to God-man in expression. The culmination is
the end result of man's union with God while in physical form, and the
spiritual consciousness of his mastery over physical principles and laws
such as gravity, time, and space. This did not imply that man, as an
evolving consciousness, would be complete and end there. In the
mastery and use of God-mind, man shall create new principles of law,
overriding past limitations in matter and manifestation.

Truly, there is no end to evolving consciousness, and yet this
dimension as an evolving schoolroom shall become obsolete to those
evolving souls who graduate into greater-dimensional classrooms. Terra,
although she is to evolve into higher-dimensional frequencies, shall still
be home to those evolving entities who come to take part in her
curriculum, even after her transformation. She shall never be a permanent home to any, for all come and go in their ever-demanding
necessity for greater unfoldment.

**When you speak of all beings in that future time as having spiritual
understanding, how can this truly be, for the world has such differ-
ing levels of belief and opinion regarding spiritual understanding?
How could an entire world come to this unity of concepts and
principles? People are at such different levels of evolvement.
Please explain this.**

Through the advanced individual and collective inner experience,
due to the increasing energies of awakening and Light, the Spirit of

oneness shall infuse the hearts and minds of all open, trusting souls and lead them into the greater knowing of Spirit's plan and purpose. All races, all cultures, all societies in their own way, in their own blessed moment, shall experience the upliftment, the opening, as these energies of higher frequency infiltrate all material Creation. Each individual, regardless of belief or religious conviction, shall experience transformation to the degree of acceptance and willingness to receive that which comes to this and all dimensions in joy, Love, and blessing.

What about those who do not accept or are not willing to receive?

They shall experience greater struggle and confusion through their willfulness to hold onto those illusionary concepts and dreams of a past dying to the now of Spirit's influx into their hearts and minds. If they persist in the fearful clutching of that which is unreal, they shall inevitably be removed from physical experience due to the sustained higher vibrations and their inability to align with them. Do not be in fear. None shall perish, for there is no death; but they shall find themselves in their proper place of life's evolving classrooms in dimensional experience. They shall, however, be lost to a wondrous opportunity for leaps in advancement because they shall have passed up the moment of the advent of the Lord and the Second Coming of Christ into their hearts and minds, a most unfortunate choice indeed, if they so choose.

You spoke of being able to commune with other species and animals through thought. Please expand on this.

All life forms communicate on different levels of vibratory thought and consciousness imaging that are easily accessible when properly understood and applied with consciousness states of altered and subtle perception. From the animal kingdom to the plant kingdom, all of created expression uses its own ways and means of skillfully communicating. The separation of conscious communication with various kingdoms rests simply in the inability to perceive those vibrational forms or aspects of projection in proper understanding and in principles of thought waves and structure. Once realized and understood in harmony and oneness all easily be able to communicate in corresponding

t vibration. As with dimensional alteration and shifts,

ed through the alignment of thought-wave frequency

...sponding species through spiritually accessing those subtle forms and levels, using inner sensitivities and psychic awareness of perception. This will be accomplished as the individual simply attunes, through these inner avenues of awareness, to the level of vibrational imagery transmitted by the particular animal, plant, or bird, and allows the reception and transmission to take place. There are those who, at this time, are able to commune with other life forms, although their numbers are few. After the dawn of Spirit's entry, however, these gifts shall be commonplace and accessed by all in the evolution of higher consciousness upon Terra.

Will there be education in the future as we now know and understand it via schools and universities?

Yes, there will be education but it will not be presented through the process that has been used in the past because the priorities of truth and the values of the inner understanding of spiritual unfoldment within man shall take precedence over the past focus of worldly, intellectual reasoning. Much of that which has been taught in your learning institutions has been useless to Humanity's search for meaning. In fact, it has added to the confusion of the true purpose of life. In the future, the knowledge and acquisition of man's union with God-self shall be paramount above all else, and the purpose for greater understanding shall not be motivated by fear or the latent desire to achieve greater social status, or wealth, or to secure a "good job."

The motivation for all education shall be to unite the individual with the Infinite Power within, and to reveal the collective advancement of man's creative nature united with God.

Classes shall be held outdoors whenever possible by higher Light teachers. Subjects taught shall be widely varied, yet each shall deal with the joyful aspects of being and the furtherance of the individual's realization of his highest potential through loving support and inner attunement. Subjects would include higher perception techniques for dimensional alteration through focused thought; chakra balancing and energizing; inner and outer healing; transformational tools and techniques; practical methods for soul or astral projection; meditation; visualization; and higher mind states. These and many other subjects shall be part of tomorrow's curriculum in the education of the soul upon Terra.

Since harmony shall be the intent and motivating factor, all subjects shall be given freely without cost, as money shall be part of your dream in your history. All subjects shall be for the benefit of the unified hearts and minds of all concerned. It shall be very much like the classes you attend even now in your dream state or in higher dimensions of being when you find yourself upon those planes of experience where you are taught about the expansion into Light.

The evolution of consciousness is the only true education, because too much focus has been placed upon the intellect and not enough on the whole of Humanity and the alleviation of its sorrows through separation from its true oneness state in awareness. In the aftermath of Spirit's awakening, education shall finally be used for its true goal of leading each soul to its own mastery of spiritual knowledge.

How may we speed up the process of awakening to our own God-self?

By realizing and believing that you are already one with your God-self, and that you are already perfect within your inner truth and being. One cannot place definitions and boundaries about oneself and say what is correct and what is not and hope to realize one's unlimitedness. When you begin your quest for self-understanding, in your zeal, you place restrictions upon yourself as to what should or should not be according to your own perception of that which is the "spiritual way" and that which is not.

Yet, I say to you that all is Spirit, all is Divine, and all ways are correct for they lead you home if you are truly present within the nowness of Love within your being. There are no absolutes for God is all things. Being all things leaves an infinite number of paths open to His heart. Walk the path that is closest to your heart, walk it in joy, and it shall surely lead you home.

There is no sure way or path that shall speed up your process of awakening for that is God's grace in action of enlightenment within you. There are those methods of which I have already spoken such as meditation, loving yourself, forgiving yourself, visualizing your own expansion into Light, and others that shall aid you in letting go of fear and limitation. These two foes block your clear perception of your own truth.

Awakening is but the releasing of belief in the illusion of your self-created dream. It is opening up your inner eyes to the truth of yourself in Spirit oneness beyond the dream of third-dimensional existence. Awakening is but the first step in your Spirit understanding and your own growth therein, yet it is your greatest step. Your first step into Spirit awareness reveals to you your potential power in oneness with Infinite Mind and your own limitless, eternal presence, thereby bestowing freedom to you in its wake. This is just the beginning, for you must still learn of its uses. You must practice in even greater degree until your mastery is won upon all aspects within yourself.

In this very moment, you are at one with your own enlightenment and awakened soul, and yet your belief in your separation, in illusion prevents you from this knowingness. Rid yourself of your beliefs, all beliefs, and rely on the trusting hand of the Father Principle within to speed you on your way to His heavenly kingdom within. All will be well with you. Let go of the shoulds and should nots, the right ways and the wrong ways. Allow yourself the freedom to walk in joyous laughter in the direction that suits your heart, and you shall find your God straight away within your loving, momentous now!

Where there is fear, there can be no trust, for fear continues belief in separation. In contrast, trust allows all good to come your way in unity of life's purpose with God's Plan and Will. Dispel fear, and you shall create greater trust. Love shall flow like a great fountain within your being, spilling outward upon all who come your way.

Trust is but inner knowing that all that is of your greater good shall indeed find you open to receive in acceptance and faith. Trust is letting go of that which has bound you to your definitions of reality and practicality. Trust allows the Divine hand of intervention to intercede and carry you across the river's raging torrents of fearfulness, knowing that all shall be well, all shall be made whole. Trust is but another way of saying that you are loving yourself enough to not place limits on your own infinite Spirit. Trust is realizing the senseless futility of relying on the rational ego personality and its lack of true perception to choose your path. Trust is going directly to your God-self and proclaiming, "Father-God within, I trust that your Divine Hand shall lead me in the way of my greatest good, and that your Will and Infinite Love shall see me through to the Light of my own awakening. I trust you now and always for my safety, for my being is secure within You and I know that You and I are one, forever. So be it."

Walk in the way of your heart in God's presence and awaken unto your Light, your self.

Are you saying to just let go of trying to control our path and allow life to lead us through it, trusting that we shall end up where we should be? That seems so haphazard.

Let go of your belief that your limited ego perception, through intellectual, rational thought, is sufficient and indeed wise enough to lead you in the direction of your greatest unfoldment. Your ego self longs to control all of your experiences and situations, and yet, in your experience, can you honestly proclaim its correctness in leading you to greater understanding? No, because it seeks to rule. As long as you give it its lead, it shall pull you along, using its tools of fear, doubt, and distrust, thereby continuing the separation of your knowingness of oneness with your own God-self.

Trusting is simply getting out of your own way, placing your ego and fear aside, and allowing a greater, Divine Hand to shape your destiny by aligning your will with it in trust and reliance.

Man's sole dependence on his ego personality has prevented him all along from his own greater self-perception in trust. It will continue to be this way until he recognizes a greater power working within him, and he turns his trust over to it, allowing it to lead him onward and upward in Light. Place your trust, therefore, in the true reality within, and follow those inner promptings and feelings which spring from your joy, knowing that they are the signposts directing you in the right course of your life's purpose toward expansion.

You are always where you should be in experience, through your self-created belief! Change your concepts of limitation, and you shall find yourself walking a new path, a path filled with greater understanding of your own truth. Dispel your fears and replace them with trust in the divinity of all-knowing wisdom within, a wisdom much greater than your intellect could ever fathom. Then follow that inner voice of insight to your own awakening within God.

Could you speak on the subject of self-discipline? It seems we all want to change but have a difficult time with disciplining ourselves to break old habit patterns.

This is extremely important if one is to advance upon the path to enlightenment and be successful. This applies as well for any venture upon the physical plane, for without self-discipline, one's days are lived out of balance and out of purpose with those greater goals which are laid out for the destiny of each soul by the higher self or oversoul.

Discipline is but another name for self-love. It means that the individual Loves himself enough to commit to change, seeking a higher purpose or direction. It means that the individual is willing to follow through and become those greater aspects of his being.

Self-discipline, or "the practice of becoming," is essential upon every aspect of living because it brings the energies of desire and will into focus and clarity. It drives the messages of success and fruition home to the subconscious levels of mind, thereby creating the desired change or upliftment. In whatever area of self-expansion or improvement, self-discipline is the key to the continued practice of self-determination of your goals and expression within form. Self-discipline should be practiced with a loving, open heart in understanding that with its practice, you are reaching greater heights within yourself and within your experience. If it is done with disdain or with an attitude of guilt, pressure, or ego attachment, your results will be unrewarding because the true purpose shall go unseen and unknown. If you discipline yourself out of your love for yourself and your greater good, you shall take leaps and bounds in your strides toward self-understanding. Discipline yourself and your time in periods of meditation, fasting, proper breathing and diet, and you shall gain much in the way of your path to Light.

You spoke of fasting. Could you elaborate on its importance?

Fasting, or the abstaining from food intake, is important on a number of levels. First, the significance on the body's systems of function needs to be addressed. The body's internal organs, as well as all circulatory systems, periodically need to experience relaxation or rest periods from continuous demand to perform their duties and functions, especially in your modern day when much of what you place within your body is without nutritional value. By overtaxing your internal systems through the intake of processed foods and poor choices of nutritionless packaged foods, you increase the imbalance of your systems and invite dysfunction to come into being. Much of your illness and disease is seen to be directly caused by this ignorance of the needs of your own body. If you would truly listen to your body's wisdom, you would understand the need for certain foods.

Your deafness to your body's wisdom causes much havoc within your life. If you would begin to understand the true purpose of food, you would gain in your knowledge of how to care for your bodily temple.

The body functions and performs more efficiently on less food than more. The fallacy that we must eat until we are full, bloated, and cannot move is completely erroneous and damaging to the system. It is better to eat six small meals in one day than two large ones because the quantity taken in a large meal is extremely taxing to those systems which support your health and well-being.

Never overeat. Eat slowly with awareness of your intake. Learn of proper nutrition and food combining, and realize that your body is your temple which must be cleaned periodically.

Fasting allows the systems to relax, rejuvenate, and become stronger. By not eating, the body moves back into balance and harmony, thereby bringing energy and health to the individual organs.

If one is beginning a fast, he must be aware of the body's wisdom and move slowly or as he feels comfortable. At first, the body, which is used to getting what it wants, will demand certain foods. As the fast continues, however, its demand will be for "any food," and if continued, you shall begin to realize that your body's demands and appetite are under control and will. Your strength and inner knowing shall increase as the realization that you are greater than your body is seen and understood.

The true purpose of fasting is not only to cleanse the inner systems and organs but also to exercise and discipline your will and become strong within your understanding that you are the Spirit and not the body. The modern man is a mere puppet of his desires and appetites of the flesh and knows little of his Divine nature. Through the practice of fasting periodically, man may begin to break the mold which holds him to his limiting concept that he is the body.

The Spirit within seeks to gain your awakening. If you are a slave to your body's demands, you shall not see your own unlimited qualities or expand beyond the views of physical desires and your enslavement therein.

Fasting done with the right intent shall be of service to you on your path of unfoldment. Therefore, practice, learn, and listen to your body's wisdom. Realize that you are the master, and expand yourself into health, Light, and joy. Educate yourself as there is much written of this subject. Through your self-discipline, it shall prove to be of great benefit to you on all levels of experience.

Can too much fasting be harmful?

As with all things, moderation is suggested. Each individual must be aware of and in tune with his body's knowing. Harm comes only when one is not listening to or aware of what is being said, and one attempts to do more than what the body can handle. Good, common sense is important to spiritual understanding because one must be in this dimension as well. Those laws which apply to your body's care should not be overlooked.

Attune yourself to your body's energies, and through fasting in the proper amount, you shall gain understanding of your own periods of rest, abstinence, and the correct application therein.

Questions and Answers about Death

How may one release his fears of death? It is easy to get caught up in the old thoughts of fearfulness because we do not really know what will be or what will take place after we die, or if we will truly survive it.

Your fears, as with all fears, are self-created, and often they are not your own but are borrowed from your parents, society and the mass social acceptance of reality. They are sustained in this pool of darkness and continue to plague your hearts and minds. This continues the drama of loss, pain, and emotional heartbreak.

If you could bear witness to the truth of your own endlessness and your survival of death transition, you would be overjoyed at your unlimited freedom in the nowness of your life. Truly, your nows are forever and are your gift from the Creator Mind. The fears which hinder your understanding are useless trash that must be discarded before you can perceive the truth of your foreverness.

What is it that you truly fear? Is it your own destruction or the loss of your identity? Is it the loss of someone dear whom you love? Or is it change and the uncertainty of the next moment?

Your identity is secure and your survival guaranteed or I would not be in communion with you now, would I? I am proof of the continuation and evolution of conscious experience outside of physical matter. My thoughts are intact, my purpose is direct, and my identity is secure within the Spirit Mind of the Father, even as are you and all of Humanity. I am no different from you except that I know who I am in oneness with the God of my being, and I am no longer focused within form. Yet you and I are one in Spirit, now and always, as are all beings.

I would boldly state that the fear of death by the masses is the fear of an uncertain tomorrow, the same fear that limits beings from becoming all that they can be. Death is yet another name for change. Many beings fear change because it disrupts the stability of the life that they seek to control and manipulate. Security and stability can never be found in a dimension of matter where change and evolution are the key to expansion.

Just as the seed must germinate and evolve into the flower, or the baby into an adult, change is ever happening on all levels of dimensional experience, for it must. Evolution is our gift and our joy for it allows us the freedom of movement, newness and foreverness that inspires the creative aspects of living, whether within form or not.

Death is the great liberator of change. It does not bring an uncertain, fearful future but offers a newer, more expansive, hope-filled now.

It is quite unthinkable for one to fancy a world of no change, no transition or evolutionary growth, because the Lord God of your being is ever in motion, constant in His eternal nature, ever creative, enhancing all life and experience with the Light of His being. Just as the plant must reach upward to the warm rays of the sun for nurturing and growth, so must the human Spirit ever reach upward in evolution to the loving arms of the Father in constant movement of all that He is, in grace, harmony, and Light.

Therefore, love your changes, love your nows, be present and aware within this moment. You shall then see your fears of an uncertain tomorrow disappear in the knowing present presence of Spirit and your safety therein.

What does it really feel like to die?

It feels like a warm breeze lovingly caressing your soul, lifting you up and away from the cares of your dream in flesh. Gently and easily, you simply slip out from your encasement and become aware of yourself outside your body form. At times, the grace of the transition is such that its swiftness and ease take the soul by surprise. As the soul views the shell and realizes it is still alive and well outside of physical reality, it is soon comforted by the Light of warm, higher energies of guidance and the unconditional loving presence of the God-self within. This is usually seen as a bright, shining, radiant Light of blinding white and golden rays which infuse the soul with its Infinite Love. Truly, the feeling of dying to the flesh form is being born back into the unlimitedness of your

Divine heritage in Spirit. The blessing of the transition is indeed a newfound freedom unto joy. The simple process of leaving behind the useless physical shell and moving into the vastness of Spirit is, in fact, much easier than the process of birth.

At birth, the soul must condense the vast omnidimensional being-ness and focus itself into the limitation of physical, structured form. To a great number of entities, this is quite distressing because the denseness of form seems to be so confining and with boundaries. The soul, in its journey back upon the physical plane, must learn again of the limiting aspects of third-dimensional experience. It must gather those lessons which are valuable in its quest for self-expansion while in form. The process of focusing the unlimited self into and upon the physical system of reality is indeed quite fascinating and complex, requiring, for the most part, higher aid and guidance from those loving guides and entities of lofty vibratory knowingness.

Aid and higher guidance are offered unto you at every point of experience in all dimensions and are at your beck and call instantaneous-ly as your desires and needs command. Therefore, be at peace, for you are ever in good hands. Be comforted within your heart and mind because God's Love is with you always.

In this world, sometimes we feel so alone in our struggle and pain. How can we overcome this empty feeling and know that we have help and truly are not alone?

One must extend oneself in the world of form and reach out to others in trust and Love, knowing that in the sharing of oneself with others, the returns will be there for one's support and emotional fulfillment. If, in your reaching, the expectation is for personal gain, or if your intent is self-centered, the returns will be few. Yet, if in your reaching, you come with an open heart and in trust, your returns shall be great. Upon the world of form, as upon higher dimensions, your heart is truly seen and your intentions felt. If you believe that you are alone, you are mistaken in your perception, for you are never alone upon this dimension, nor on any other, for that matter, as we are all one in Spirit Essence and universal Mind. The separation of individual consciousness occurs as the entity perceives and believes in his aloneness and separation from the One and from all others. The separation is simply illusion and non-understanding of the truth that we are all very much connected in Spirit and in consciousness.

If one, in his anxiety of aloneness, were to but ask for that which he desired and then acted upon the desire by extending himself outward into the world in trust and knowing that the God of his being would be delivering the desire, he would indeed receive that which he asked for. One must ask if one is to receive. One must be clear in his desire for proper manifestation to occur. Your focused desire, with clear intent and trust in the receiving of it, shall bring your wish to you. You must ask and extend yourselves outward to the world in faith, and trust that all things are yours already.

Your Spirit friends are ever with you and desirous of your knowingness of Spirit in loving connection. They work and wait for your consciousness to open to receive all of the support and gentle guidance they have to offer. It is up to you to realize your wondrous oneness with all life forms. Take comfort in the knowledge that within God's Infinite Kingdom, all are Love, all are cared for, all are held within His Eternal Thought.

So be it! May all of Humanity come to the realization of their oneness of being with all of God's Creation. May they banish forever the separation of consciousness and the illusion of fearful thought.

You are truly never alone for your God is ever with you and about you, ever waiting for recognition.

How may one learn to love oneself?

Within your world, the limitation of thought and lack of perception of the true nature of self prevails. Your fearful concepts and beliefs prevent you from clearly viewing the loving, vibrant power of which you are a part. You cannot love that which you do not perceive or know. Since your birth, you have been told and programmed in limiting concepts of yourself. The illusion of your dream continues because you cannot see yourself as you truly are. Your parents, guides, and outer social structure of thought have told you that you are your personality, looks, talent, abilities, behavior, body, intelligence, and on and on, yet none of these characteristics is the true you. They are but the outward reflection in form of the inner, true reality within you. You are much greater, more capable, and perfect within your being than you presently know. You are the Creator Spirit within. That is truly what is to be cherished, loved, and held in highest honor and respect, for you are a necessary spark of the whole of God's Creative Thought. In reality, there is no separation from you and your God-self. It exists only in your sleep of illusion and unawareness of your own truth.

You must begin to let go of the old, worn-out fears and beliefs which restrict your knowing of your true self. As these are released, your Love shall grow, for your Light within shall shine brightly for you to see. As your inner self is perceived more and more closely and clearly, your love of self shall expand as well, until one day, you shall awaken to such joy, such bliss of understanding, that your heart and soul shall fly to the heavens of God's limitless expanse, and you shall be free!

You say that we do not love ourselves because we do not really see and know who and what we are. If it is true that we are living in an illusion and have false beliefs about what we are and that our real self within goes unseen and unknown, how may we dispel this illusion, this false dream in which we are asleep? How may we really know ourselves?

Your attention and awareness have been placed upon your outer world, your outer reality. You have been taught that all which is valid and worthy of your energy and focus is that which takes place outside of yourself. Your inner self and inner truth go unnoticed. Because of this, your life is lived haphazardly and out of balance. Without understanding that your inner being actually creates your outer experiences and seeming reality, your true power is unused, and you are left at the mercy of life's turbulence and uncertainty. As long as your focus is placed outside of yourself instead of on your true inner reality, you shall experience the emptiness, the separation, and the misidentification with all that is your true nature. As long as this continues, you shall not perceive yourself and thereby learn of your own loving being, which is your God-self in expression.

Your illusion consumes you. The continued belief patterns structure your outer reality. Your outer reality reinforces the validity of your beliefs and fearful thoughts, even though these beliefs are self-created. This causes the endless cycle of outer reality, which is created through inner belief, to continue. Like layers of clothing which cover your body, this prevents you from perceiving your own true inner being.

To know yourself and cease identifying yourself with your body, thoughts, outer reality or circumstances, possessions, relationships, or any and all things outside of your being, look within yourself for your own truth. Stop responding to or relying on opinions of others as to your own worth or value. Cease depending upon anyone or anything outside yourself for your own self-love or fulfillment. Dive deep within the ocean of your being and discover the priceless wisdom of God-self. Through this, you shall know yourself. Through this knowingness, you shall love all that you are.

Begin today, now, to let go of those rigid thought patterns which you label as yourself. Go beyond your own created limits to view your true, loving, gentle self. Forgive yourself for all that you have believed to be evil or in error, and realize that your real self is beyond any and all acts in the drama of life. Realize that you are forever perfect and blessed in the totality of non-judgment and unconditional Love.

When we speak of loving one's self, we refer not to the ego personality, for this is ever changing and transitory and not of the eternal changelessness of Spirit. We refer to the true self, which is constant Love, Light, and wisdom of which each is a part. The greater self within is your true nature, your true character, your true home, and that which is to be loved and felt.

When you perceive yourself, your thoughts are usually self-critical or self-defeating, with judgments and condemnation for behavior that you have perceived, through your belief system, to be wrong. However, these are only beliefs in what is right and wrong, and not in the truth of that which is. Your reality and beliefs are your truth. In the greater perspective, however, all is seen to be part of the dream of this illusionary world of form which holds your mind tightly, keeping it from seeing the larger understanding that all truth, all experience, all reality is self-created.

When you truly know that your patterns of thought and belief concepts choose your destiny as well as your present reality, then you shall begin to view the power which resides within the creative aspects of yourself. You then begin to choose those thoughts and concepts which will create your life anew with greater joy, Love, and Light therein!

In this moment, you must forgive yourself. Picture yourself as the perfect Light within that ever shines; that is beyond your concepts of good and bad, right and wrong; that exists beyond the drama of self-created existence. Instead, picture yourself as ever alive, vibrant, constant, loving and loved, now and always. Picture this, for in reality, it is truth, it is fact, it is your Divine heritage. As God's wondrous thought enfolds you in safety and endless continuance, you are forever part of His kingdom of peace and Love. Recognize your divinity and the kingdom of heaven within yourself, and you shall know all the bliss and wisdom that rests peacefully therein.

You must understand that there is no act in loving, for you are Love. Your very nature being Love leaves nothing to do but be the Love and Light that you are. It is a natural function of your self when fear and limitation have been dispelled. When fear and limiting concepts no longer hold your heart and mind in bondage, your loving being is free to express the nowness of Love's attributes. When an entity creates walls about him in his fear of being hurt, or in fear of that which is unseen and unknown, he prevents the natural influx and outpouring of that energy to flow in its totality, thus shutting the doors to higher perception and greater learning. Joy and Love go hand in hand, and the oneness of yourself with God-Spirit produces this joy and Love naturally, and your unfoldment increases. Would you not rather have a life filled with joy, Love, and trust than a life experiencing fear and lack of fulfillment? The only true fulfillment is to be found in Love, true Love, Love which knows no boundaries or limits, Love which is eternal, ever evolving and ever present within you. That Love shall be awakened as you lay down your fears along with the old perceptions of that which is real or worthy. Openly accept now your own perfect, loving nature within. Become one with your knowing, and be all that you are in Love, by Love, and for Love, now and forever.

Can you speak about play and its importance in our lives which seem so serious most of the time?

Play and those activities which encourage self-acceptance, self-love, and self-expansion, and which deal with the joy of living, are wondrous gifts which bring you closer to the laughing child of God within. Those activities of play that allow your being the expansion of joyful arenas of experience are to be cultivated. You should play in your daily life as often as possible because it allows a pressure release from stress-filled activities and creates a greater balance of healing energies within the body and mind.

Allow your child within to express and be in aliveness in the joy of Creation. Bring more play into your life, along with more fun, more laughter, and carefree enjoyment. This shall prove to be a balm of sweet elixir which shall soothe the aching soreness of your seriousness in your daily stress-filled life.

The purpose is to also aid you in the heightening of your vibratory field, because as your play is in process, the density and heaviness of frequency is thrown off and released on deeper levels. Through your laughter, which is truly the elixir of life, the joy of your being sends to your body centers and glands the message of lightness, mirth, and cheer. That message is processed directly through subtle secretions, both physical and etheric, and then dispatched throughout your body, giving forth healing, balancing, and harmonizing qualities which enhance your health and longevity, your mind's peace and equanimity, and your Spirit's bonding with both of these.

Love your life, your work, your play, and yourself, for in that lovingness, your vibrational alteration will indeed be quickened greatly. You shall then skip and run to your Father's arms in happy mirthfulness of Spirit. So be it.

If we come from the heart, and our will is linked with God's Will, can we then do anything, and it will be in alignment with God's plan

and purpose?

Yes, for the God of your being is within your heart and your Love. If all that you say or do comes from that place of Love, it shall be expressed in the perfection of your highest self. Your highest self is that aspect of perfection, the all-knowing spark of God-Mind, eternally wise and infinitely powerful. To express your highest being is the destiny of all God's children upon Terra. To be at one with your highest aspect of being is to express yourself in joy and creativity in all that you do. The goal is to align yourself in totality through the releasing of your old concepts and beliefs and to allow your higher mind complete expression. That is joining your will with God's Will and the ultimate path of creating heaven within yourself and your world.

If you were one with your highest self, you could not perform an act of transgression or manifest unkind results. It simply would not be within your nature. The higher mind would perceive all possible outcomes and probable parallel realities. Choices would be instantaneously relayed to you in perfect order and timing so that the most advantageous, opportune decisions would be available to you. Your first intuitive insight is the correct one as to any and all inner perceptual decisions. Your trust in your higher mind to give you all that you need is paramount when choosing correctly for the greatest possible results.

All things work for the highest good, however, even when it is that you perceive in judgment what seems to be imperfect or wrong. That is why we urge you to connect with your highest being, because your intellect is incapable of seeing the expanded picture of what may be your best direction. Follow your joy! Come from the heart, and you shall be following the directing wisdom of the highest-self, linked with God.

You have spoken before about the Brotherhood of Light and how it works with other forces of Light from other dimensions, including extraterrestrial entities. Could you speak more of this?

We indeed work together in closeness of purpose with many beings collectively for the advancement of higher vibratory awakening and the shift of dimensional expansion. The inter- and extradimensional entities, as well as extraterrestrial intelligences of Light, are united in this task. In this quest, we utilize all necessary information and advanced intelligence offered by them. The extraterrestrials are both within and around Terra at this time. They are free to come and go at their discretion, usually placing themselves in those areas from which they can transmit significant data to those open, receptive channels for the furtherance of their purpose. They are both incarnate and out of body. Some choose only to create an omnidimensional physical form for a short duration to suit their objectives. They are from many galaxies, both distant and near, and seek to form greater communication with mankind. They work for man's inevitable acceptance of their reality and his awakening to transpire into higher consciousness states. They function on various dimensional planes and are able to accomplish technological miracles through their scientific approach. They utilize advanced intelligence to such a great degree as to humble the most astute Earth scientist. They are able to traverse physical dimensions through the use of universal, grid-like patterns, or quadrants, and shift to light-frequency thought, thereby transporting themselves and their ships to far reaches of planetary space instantaneously.

The beings who are interdimensional are many, as well, existing upon parallel worlds of form and nonform within different vibratory frequencies. You would be amazed at the endless number of vibratory worlds of Creation and life which exist parallel to your own. Countless myriads of fascinating beings and worlds are living and expressing their dimensional lives right where you are sitting at this very moment. You do not see them for they are of higher vibration and therefore invisible to your senses. Yet, they do exist, and are quite real.

The vast forces of intelligent, wise entities gathered now within this sector of the galaxy are truly quite astounding. Their presence assures the unification and ultimate success of our collective mission. This dimension shall shift into its higher frequency, and mankind shall awaken. The individual must choose for himself when he shall accept the Light into his mind and life, however, and that is why we work within the hearts and consciousness of those who are stirring in their sleep. We nudge them in Spirit to open their eyes and perceive the radiance within them.

Now, in your world, the call is being proclaimed for the dream of illusion to end and the Father-God Principle to claim his throne and power within each consciousness. The moment of your awakening is at hand. Oh Humanity, harken to the call!

How does one rise above the karmic chain? It seems we are driven by past patterns that are carried over from other lifetimes, and we choose certain situations over and over again. How can we break this cycle?

You can do this by being in the now of the moment in your experiences and by being aware of your feelings, desires, and motivations. In other words, become inquisitive about all aspects of yourself, and discover what causes your patterns of fear, guilt, and those continued dramas of your experience within your life. Your evolving awareness seeks answers to many questions, but you overlook that which is happening right within yourself and thus continue the cycles of pain and separation. The movement of your consciousness to grow beyond the karmic wheel ultimately shall be reached when your consciousness merges with the Father-God Principle. Until that revealing experience occurs within you, take hold of your present experience, your present moment, and be as completely in that moment as possible within your thoughts, actions, and perceptions. Whenever fear thought forms arise within your mind, be aware and flow with them to their cause within your experience.

Meditate upon those areas of your life which are out of balance and where disharmony occurs. Trace your inner experience back upon your life and past lives through Akashic attunement to discover the initial cause of your pattern, whatever it may be. Discover yourself on all levels of being, and you shall realize that all that has occurred, all experiences brought forth, have had definite purpose and meaning for you and your learning process. Bless all experiences and situations be they adverse or joyous, for they are all wise and loving teachers for you. Seek not, therefore, to rise above your karma, but seek to know yourself in all ways. Through that knowing, realize your oneness with All That Is. Through this, you shall leave behind your patterns of enslavement.

When we are faced with problems that seem so overwhelming, and we feel we cannot decide which way to turn, how can we come back to our center and regain our balance?

The life experience within this dimension of learning requires that each individual consciousness come to the ultimate knowing of its own power and strength. Adversity and painful situations or decisions all serve to awaken you to that inner reservoir of infinite wisdom and power. Without them, you would not have cause to discover your own inner strength. It is true that when you are face to face with problems, you sometimes allow the fear of past programming to overshadow your inner balance, and you fall into confusion and despondency.

When this happens, you must, first and foremost, return to now! Look calmly at the complete picture as much as possible, and breathe deeply and slowly. Move through your fear thoughts. As your breath begins to calm, your thoughts also shall become calm, allowing you access to clarity of vision and understanding of issues and aspects related to the correct choice to be made. Allow your inner wisdom full authority, and listen to that advice or direction offered through your inner senses. Receive the insight information, and then act upon your true feelings as to your path.

Your balance shall be restored as soon as the fear thoughts are allowed their freedom, and the clarity of vision shall return through calmly breathing and attuning to your inner wisdom.

Do not hesitate to ask for guidance and assistance from the higher realms for it is always available to you when you need help. Guidance and valuable information shall flow through your consciousness at the moment of asking.

When the fearful moment is over, reflect upon the fear that overwhelmed your mind, and trace it back in your life and earlier times. Then reflect upon the situation and how it mirrored your belief and fear pattern, thus presenting your lesson. This is how you shall overcome your patterns and ultimately achieve inner freedom and knowledge of yourself.

You say we should allow the fearful thoughts their freedom, but how will we ever rid ourselves of their power if we let them come in?

Wisdom is not gained through suppression but through allowing the fearful thoughts their moment of expression, flowing with them in awareness and perceiving their effects upon your body and mind. As your awareness shifts to the inner understanding of the fundamental reason for the fear, which is usually due to past experiences of pain, loss, or hardship, you shall be more capable of recognizing those situations that mirror your fearful beliefs. You can then begin to release them from your being. Once fear is allowed to disappear through your own wisdom and understanding of the cause of your anxiety, you shall experience a new freedom and shall not be plagued again by that particular issue. One must not attempt to deny or hold back those thoughts based in fear issues because they are your teachers. Your lessons shall not be learned and overcome if you bury your head in the sands of ignorance and illusion. Face your fear thoughts in courage. Understand that they are part of your illusion and bondage to your dream, and are not your greater reality. Give them their say, yet recognize that your power and Light are all-wise and capable of dispelling them forever through your own knowing, expanding self.

Why do we speak so often of breaking free of your illusion? Why do we say that your joy and Light are beyond this dream which you have created? This is because all dreams have their beginning and ending. All plays have their first act and last act. All of physical Creation experiences birth and death, day and night, sickness and health, joy and sorrow. There are always the spectrum of opposites and the poles of ever-changing phenomena which capture the consciousness in a web of seeming reality, yet, in the end, offer only death.

True reality, the reality which we wish for you to know and experience, is eternal, forever, ever-blissful, and filled with Light and Love. True reality, that which every soul deeply wants, can be found only within one's own being and truth. That is the final lesson to be learned upon Terra in order for mankind to take his next step into Godhood. All else is but a dream, an illusion that shall one day pass away. Your body is born unto this plane, and one day you must leave it behind, yet your true reality shall remain within the perfection of its beingness long after your present form has turned to dust. Reflect upon this as you move through your life. All that you see and perceive about you with your present physical senses shall one day turn to dust upon your world of form. All the people who are inhabiting bodies shall one day be gone from them. All the objects such as automobiles and homes, all those things outside of yourself that you have given power to, shall indeed, at some future point, be no more. The consciousness locked in darkness gives power to these things and their seeming reality. The wise being sees them for what they are, uses them for learning, yet gives power and validity to the true reality within, the unborn, undying Spirit-self. All things on Earth shall pass away, but your self is forever. Reflect upon this for it indeed is a great truth. Give your acknowledgement to that which deserves it — your true inner being. View all things in your world as but tools for learning or the acquisition of wisdom, but know yourself as the one and only reality.

You say that we are already perfect within our higher selves. Why do you say that we need to expand and evolve if we are already all-knowing, all-powerful beings of perfection?

You are upon form within this dimension of illusion and seeming separation, yet, in greater knowing, you are never separate but are one eternally with your highest God-self. We speak of expansion from the perspective of your present conscious awareness and acceptance of your dream illusion as being reality. There is the need to raise your perception and consciousness to the state of being wherein you shall perceive yourself in truth as an unlimited being.

Yes, at this very moment, you are perfect. Yet, you are unaware, unknowing of your perfection because the illusion of your dream reality is still in control within your beliefs and concepts of reality. When your consciousness expands to accept and receive that inner wisdom of truth, you shall indeed view yourself as eternally perfect, whole, and in complete harmony with All That Is. It is your limited concepts which bind you to the phenomenal world of form and which dictate to your mind the seeming validity of your judgments of self and the imperfections therein. Once you perceive and know your true self, all else shall be seen for what it truly is — illusion!

The process of expansion into Light is simply your awakening into true reality from the ignorance of sleep and the dream of your illusion. Yet, within the greater truth, you are ever perfect, now and always. Your task is to realize this truth within you. There is nothing you can say or do that shall alter this fact, for truth is eternal, and you are the truth.

The process of evolution and the expanding self is one in which we allow our consciousness to perceive more of the totality of our own truth and Light. Being All That Is, and being ever eternal, yet expanding into greater self-knowing, we share in the joyful experience of ourselves in greater and greater acceptance, allowance, and trust of the Love, joy, and wisdom which we are. Blissful states of being and consciousness are ever expanding and elevate in intensity as we align in greater oneness with the Light of our being within God's thought.

Evolution simply means coming home to ourselves in greater and greater degrees. Do you believe me when I say to you that all the joy, bliss, and truth that you shall ever truly experience and know are right within you now and always? If not, then know that you are still locked within your dream and have not yet awakened, for your knowingness is yet in slumber, asleep to your own truth. Look outside yourself for all that you desire, and you shall never find the answer or the truth. You have been doing this during all of your lifetimes, and to no avail, for you are still here, within the drama of your dream, and still asleep to yourself.

It is time now to look within yourself for all the Love, joy, and bliss that you have longed for, lifetime upon lifetime, incarnation after incarnation. See your truth, see yourself, and realize your oneness in Spirit, now and forever.

Jonathon, specifically, what is the difference between soul and Spirit?

The term "Spirit," as used in our communication with you, could be described as the ever-pervading essence of energy which is accessed, used, and is part of all materialized form and nonmaterial Creation. An analogy would be your electricity, whereby one plugs an apparatus into the main source of it to receive that spark-of-life activation. It is a crude analogy but one we must offer. Energy, or Spirit, is always present and accessible in order for all life forms to exist. All of Creation is empowered by this force for life and experience. The difference between electricity and Spirit is that Spirit can never be unplugged because it is always prevalent and part of your life force.

Continuing the analogy, the soul would be compared to the individual unit that is plugged into the main socket receiving the energy. The soul, or individual essence of energy, is indeed part of all other units or individuals because it relies upon that same force to empower it and infuse it with life-giving sustenance. In other words, the soul, or individual unit of growing expansion, although seemingly separate, is tied to and is one with all other units of consciousness, but it remains alone and separate until it is able to perceive its oneness state through the process of unfolding understanding.

The soul is the individual unit of expression in evolution, and the Spirit is the all-pervading, ever-perfect, constant source of life. The question arises that if all individual souls are seemingly progressing to an ultimate awareness of themselves, and, at the same time, are the substance of Spirit perfection, how can these two ideas exist simultaneously? How can the soul and the Spirit be a part of and intrinsic to each other?

First, without the knowledge that all life is supported and sustained by Spirit Principle, it is difficult to grasp the concept that individual consciousness is tied to a greater fundamental, universal mind, or that all thought is part of a larger perspective since each soul entity, being a thought of the Creator Mind, is able to function seemingly independently and free of the greater Source Mind. In truth, it does not, because all are connected and intertwined in cosmic oneness.

The illusion remains for each individual consciousness that it is separate from the whole, or the Source, until it is able to see that the truth of its wholeness with All That Is has indeed never been unplugged from the source of itself. In other words, you perceive yourself in your understanding as an individual soul until you realize that you are much greater than the individual unit of separate consciousness. Then you shall know through cosmic alignment that all along, you were always the ocean and not merely the wave. You have always been Spirit, yet, in the bondage of illusion, you have viewed yourself as the unit that must be plugged in to receive the truth when, in reality, you are the truth, you are the reason for being; you are "being" itself.

You are truly the All, and the All is Spirit essence. Until your self-expanded state is known, you shall see duality and separation. If we were to tell you at this moment that all is so simple and so easy to understand, you might not believe it.

Please, my wondrous brothers and sisters, do not search outside of yourself in terms and definitions. There are no terms or definitions in Spirit because Spirit simply is. I Am that I Am! The experience of being is so utterly simple, and yet, the separation of man's consciousness with the preoccupation of duality continues for he seeks all outside of himself.

If indeed all rests within you, what need is there of intellectual pursuit for the many answers that are not answerable through mental means? How does it serve you to satisfy your intellect in the moment and yet have your heart still hunger for a greater perception? If you would truly perceive the loving, all-knowing essence of which you are a part and with which you are intimately connected, you must cease your intellectual games, mental gymnastics, and the relentless pursuit of truth through doctrine and theology.

Instead, seek your own realization by turning within yourself for Light and greater awakening. In the end, even we can but point the way because the road must be walked by you alone. We are but guides on your journey home. Our words are merely words. Your experience must be felt within you and your knowing must be your own if you are to truly be a Light unto yourself and others.

I say to you now that you are the truth, the way, and the Light, yet you do not believe me for you search here and there, giving away your power and strength to others of seemingly greater knowledge; yet you are the master and the Lord God of your being. You see yourself as powerless, frail, unable to create your life, and you allow others to create it for you.

Cease this! Stand erect, stand tall in the knowledge that you are forever. You have at your command All That Is if you will but ask in loving awareness of your oneness with God's power and Light. See that you are at one with your Source, and that you are truly part of a greater energy which animates your body. That greater energy observes your thoughts and mind and experiences this dimensional schoolroom in all of its many levels. You are the creation of your dream and not merely the actor in it. Step outside of your limited creation and see the dreamer. Look behind the mirror of your eyes and see yourself, the Spirit essence that encompasses all. Connect with the ocean of your beingness first. Then all questions shall be answered, and all thoughts shall cease, for you shall be in the nowness of your experience of self. All talk and all words shall melt away into the bliss of oneness.

Understanding is fulfilled in silence. Be silent and allow the stillness to fill you with God's presence and Love, and all intellectual processes shall seem as but a game which you have played with yourself for too long.

Know yourself, and you shall be free of all misconception and misunderstanding. To know yourself is to know All That Is.

Why is there so much pain and suffering in this world? How could there be so many wars and so much evil-doing causing whole populations to be killed and towns to be destroyed?

Upon the schoolroom of Terra, mankind, in his greed and ignorance, has carried out the play of ego attachment on every level of experience. Within this drama, there have been and continue to be those who, within the darkness of their limited perceptions of themselves and the world about them, seek to enslave those whom they would control and manipulate through fear for the furtherance of their own power, wealth, and fame.

They do not perceive the temporary position of the ever-changing winds of their lives and their subsequent downfall and death in the physical. Their sole aim is to enhance their personal power. They then inflict great suffering on those whom they seek to control. Their lessons are many, yet their karmic destiny shall teach them, eventually bringing them to their own personal Light, if and when they are ready to receive it.

Yet, the question in your heart is truly how and why could an infinite, all-loving, all-powerful God allow such as these to commit such heinous crimes against Humanity? How could this God seemingly let those few, through their madness and greed, inflict such sorrow upon masses of people? What is the purpose, what is the lesson, what is the reason God does nothing to stop this madness, this insanity, this senseless pain and suffering?

All of your experiences are self-created and serve as the teachers of Humanity. The God of your being ever observes and allows you free will at all times and the free expression therein, in complete Love and acceptance of the totality of His thoughts. Thus, having this free will in expression upon your dimension of learning, all actions and choices are yours to be made as you will. The outcome, or karmic reaction, comes at the appointed time and place within your experience but is not always seen. Therefore, it would seem that these souls indeed go unscathed in their dire retribution. Yet, all is held within the Mind of the Infinite Father-God Principle, and all is within harmony and law even though it is unseen upon your plane of experience. Your God is within you and, being the silent observer, is truly that which you are.

If we begin with the principle that God is within you, as He is eternally, then all of Humanity's choices and actions are made within His Will, understanding and allowance. Why, then, would God allow such suffering? It is because God, being all things and all of Creation, is in total allowance of Himself to be all that is willed and desired to be.

If a God of vengeance and judgment of Humanity's actions were to appear in the sky and wreak havoc on the "evil doers" and reward the "good souls," would not mankind inwardly revolt at such an act? Restrictions and limitations would be placed upon your world and experience, and through those limitations, greater illusion and belief in separation of good and evil would take place. God, the God of your heart and soul, would never intervene in man's play of Creation unless invited. He comes forward now to man's heart, to man's soul and consciousness, to awaken him to his connection with the Light of his being. God allows masses of Humanity to be relieved of their physical bodies in war and cataclysm because He is within all. By being within and part of all, He allows all to be, to become, to create those lessons for themselves that will bring them greater understanding of their Spirit-soul connection.

With great suffering comes great learning examples for Humanity of the senselessness and the futility of injustice to fellow men. All create their ultimate destiny through choices and decisions made today through their free will. Those who decide to be part of a greater plan as teachers of mankind or as examples to help create a greater compassion and understanding in man do indeed at times choose to leave their bodies in great numbers, as in times of war, famine, or Earth upheaval. It would seem to man's finite understanding that there is no rhyme or reason for this loss of life, and yet, in the greater, unseen purpose of All That Is, there is a perfect path on which the Divine Mind clearly reveals to each entity his own higher purpose through those experiences of pain, hardship, and struggle on the physical plane.

There will come a day when mankind no longer makes war against his fellow man, but this will come only when man realizes the God of All is within All, and that his brother is himself in Spirit and equality.

All suffering and pain is of the dream play of physical Creation, and the Great Spirit of All allows this dream to continue for it is the play, the stage, the props, the actors, the theater, the script, all things upon the stage of life. For it to deny a part of itself through free expression would be to deny all the experience of learning and growth upon form within the play. All must be given this freedom. Imagine the great and wondrous, infinite, unconditional Love which the Father-God Principle is, to allow and give this freedom of will and expression to all upon all levels of experience. Truly, the loving Father is ever compassionate and understanding of mankind's plight and suffering, for He is all.

When viewed from the higher purpose, all things are seen to be of worth in the God-Force Principle's plan for mankind's ultimate illumination. Those experiences which are deemed evil or negative are but further lessons which man creates for himself in his growth process. Your teachers are many and powerful in your schoolroom. Learn well from those who have contributed through their pain to your awakening. Love them for their sacrifice to push you on to your deeper knowing that all are forever safe within the loving arms of the Father-Spirit. Though death may visit you in the night of your days, you shall always be within the allness of God's eternal being, now and forever.

Why, in religious teachings, are the concepts of evil, hell, damnation, Satan, and other negative concepts taught? Why is God a vengeful God? And if the Bible is divinely inspired, why are people taught these things, causing them to live in fear of a punishing God?

The control and enslavement of men's beliefs have been a requirement in all or most power-driven organizations. Those who seek to control the masses must portray and teach fear if they are to maintain that control. Within Christianity's powerful structure, fear-based beliefs play a vital role in the longevity and dominion of the Church's doctrine. Fear principles are taught to maintain its power. The concepts of dark forces and evil are simply ignorance of the Light which resides within all of God's loving thoughts. Mankind has thus created these concepts of evil through lower thought-forms of fear and hatred in separation from the God-Force Principle within.

When seen from the view of Spirit, there is no evil, for how could the Infinite Mind and Spirit which is part and parcel of all That Is be a negative or evil thing? Evil resides within man's limited perception of himself and the world, and as with all illusions and dreams, he must one day awaken to the truth that he is God, and being God is all good, all loving, and all wonderful. Again, it is the belief in good and evil that continues the drama of the illusion. God is all things, and being all things, He would not, could not wreak vengeance and eternal damnation upon any entity for committing evil through ignorance of his divinity and foreverness. God could not and would not condemn Himself.

All things being Spirit-essence are forever thoughts within the Eternal Mind of God and are eternally evolving, alive, vibrant, radiant and pure. It does not matter that one, through ignorance and lack of understanding, turns to seemingly evil ways, because his lessons are self-created and his actions will reap their just rewards in present or future incarnations. Ultimately, truth shall prevail, and inner understanding shall be revealed to each entity as he opens and awakens to his true God-self connection.

The Bible, which was written by man through Divine inspiration, was altered to fit the needs and purposes of the clergy and the Church fathers in their quest for control and superiority. Many of the teachings of Jesus were omitted or changed because he taught concepts such as reincarnation and the foreverness of the Spirit of man. In order to quell the zeal of those who rejoiced in the knowledge that they had infinite time and lives to experience their evolving path to their Godhood, the Church realized that it must alter this teaching. To attain ultimate control of the masses, they felt they must teach that one had but one life in which to achieve perfection, and one life only. They stated that unless one were to walk the path of Church doctrine and law, one would suffer the fate of eternal damnation and the pits of hell.

The term "hell" in the days of Christ's life and times referred to a pit where those unfortunate souls were placed outside of Jerusalem when it was their time to die, either through natural diseases such as leprosy, or as a condemned murderer. The Church merely borrowed the term used by those early mendicants to peddle fear and punishment as a means to impart fear of God's vengeance upon evil sinners.

For centuries this doctrine of fear and rigid control has enslaved the minds of men and women. This teaching has led to great confusion and misunderstanding. The teachings of Jesus were of the power of Love. Jesus taught Love for he knew himself to be Love, even as you are.

In the New Testament it is written that Jesus was tempted by the devil. If there is no devil, why was this written?

The teachings of Jesus and many writings therein cannot be viewed and understood simply through the written word but must be seen more deeply, and the symbology truly understood.

The story of Jesus' temptation by Satan was his own inner struggle with thought-forms of limitation taking place within him. The battle and frustration with the human weaknesses and fear thought-forms must be overcome by all who sincerely desire the Light and freedom of Christ Consciousness, and their ascension to higher dimensions of understanding.

The Bible sought to convey inner truths which were experienced not only by Jesus but also by Moses, Elijah, and other prophets. Much of what was written was imparted with a deeper meaning and character behind the outer words. One must perceive with eyes of Spirit that which is of Spirit, and put the intellect to rest.

The devil is man's creation to instill fear and enslave his fellow man by perceiving separation between man and God. There is no separation when perceived through the eyes of wisdom and Love. There is only Spirit-oneness, joy, and eternal Light.

Belief creates your personal reality, and that which you believe to be is your truth. Yet, in greater perception, evil is seen as the illusion it truly is — self-created, limiting, fear thought-forms.

In earlier times, the civilization of Humanity needed laws to control and create order out of the chaos of ignorant barbarism. The fear of a vengeful, angry God was the personification of man's psychological and spiritual state of evolution; thus, he created his God. As man evolves in spiritual understanding and perceives more of himself and his God union, he will create a more expanded view of the God-self until one day, belief will no longer be necessary, as the true inner knowingness of man's oneness with Infinite Spirit will be experienced and felt by all.

Your thoughts create your reality, so create wisely, oh Humanity! Create lovingly and with forgiveness of yourself and your brothers in your hearts. Think about others what you would have others think about you, for your Spirit-self is equal to the All and could never be greater than any other Divine thought in the heart of God's loving mind.

There is no eternal damnation, only eternal, evolving, Divine thought within the Infinite Mind of God's gentle embrace. Relinquish the fear of a punishing, vengeful Creator, for your fearful thoughts limit you and create your prison of enslavement within form through belief in your destruction. Truly, you are held precious and loved in the Light of your God, now and forever.

Blessed be each Divine thought which is part of God's loving mind, and may all realize the unconditional, loving presence within their hearts and cherish and love their own ever-evolving self into the Light of God's Kingdom of Heaven within. Amen.

Jonathon, how may man change and be less greedy and power-driven and see beyond this drama of his self-created fears and divisions with his God-self?

Man is indeed currently within this process as the intensifying energies of Light and expansion fill the darkness of his heart and mind, allowing greater awakening to occur. This period of Terra's awakening is truly a wondrous time because the mass shifts in consciousness shall be astounding as the past patterns of fear thought-forms are broken down, and the shift to higher levels of understanding takes place. Mankind is ready for this to occur because the greater portions of Humanity's numbers have indeed incarnated at this time to experience and be part of this process.

Those individuals who struggle and stubbornly refuse to accept the vast social, political, psychological, and spiritual challenges and alterations in consciousness and experience shall find their lives becoming increasingly more difficult. Their ability to cope shall be challenged. It is the flow of God's Light and the waves of higher energies that must be aligned with and unified in your being if you are to gracefully dance with the wondrous melodies of change. You shall bear witness to vast transformation on every level of outward, worldly structure as well as on those inner psychological, spiritual levels within you. Prepare yourself for change for it comes upon you in swiftness.

Be flexible within your mind and heart and soar with the winds of God's changing dawn upon Terra. Be at peace and know that the dream is about to end. Your birth into a new day is at hand, into a new awareness of yourself, your power, your Light, and your connection to the God of your being, All That Is.

What is the meaning of "rapture" as it is taught in Christian doctrine, and is it applicable only to certain people? When is it to occur if, in fact, it does exist?

The term "rapture," in reference to teachings and prophesies inspired by Biblical doctrine, relates to that moment when those individuals who have allowed Spirit entry into their consciousness will be gathered up into higher dimensional ecstasy and thought. However, those original concepts were manipulated and altered through man's intervention and perception of the intended doctrinal meaning. The original and intended script referred to the prophecy of the end of time, or the last days, to mankind's sleep of ignorance of his Spirit-self connection, and his subsequent awakening and opening to higher understanding. This is accompanied by the ecstacy of the rapture of God-consciousness. Beyond Christianity's limited teachings, we offer the truth and factual observation that God, the All in All, is within and a part of all mankind, and thus excludes none of his offspring in this venture due to their religious observance or philosophical bent. Only those who, in willfulness and ignorance of those loving energies of Light, refuse to partake of the ever-expanding, unfolding plan of God, shall go the way of lesser vibrational awareness and subsequently lose the opportunity of God-awareness in this life. There are no chosen people except those who either choose through their own free will to walk the path of Light or the path of darkness. Rapture, in its conceptual design, was intended to instill faith and hope in those individuals who, through eons of lifetimes, could be assured that in the final days of mankind's history, they would, if faithful and true to God's purpose, indeed experience the wondrous joy of ultimate superconsciousness and heaven within themselves. Rapture is the raising of vibratory currents to fourth- and fifth-dimensional character, incurring liberation from Maya, or the dream of self-created illusion.

The time frame of this occurrence is in process now. The world's vibrational alignment with higher energies of Light proceeds moment to moment as man's awareness exceeds his fears of past programming in limitation and self-doubt. The allotted time framework of man's understanding to unfold is within the now and shall continue to press forward until, as we see it, the approximate year of 2012, when much, if not all of Humanity still existing within physical expression shall be within the rapture and joyous states of superconscious awareness.

Will there be an Armageddon, and what is the meaning of the term?

The Armageddon referred to in the Biblical prophecies was related as being symbolic of mankind's final battle with the armies of lower thought-forms of fear in inner combat with Lighter vibratory awakening. The term meant to convey the final conflict within man's being as he struggles to free himself from the historical dream of self-delusion within form. The Battle of Armageddon is the final battle within man's soul for mastery of self and the awakening of Spirit's full potential within his consciousness.

Representative of the end times, or the last days of man's dream in flesh, Armageddon signified man's final battle for Light, truth, and Spirit understanding.

Yes, there shall be the final battle within each entity's consciousness as the lower self clashes with the higher vibrations of Love and Light, yet the battle shall bring no blood. It will birth the new God-man into awakening of himself in oneness with the God of his being.

The Biblical prophecies, although seen and taken literally by the Church councils and senior fathers, were nonetheless altered and changed by certain influential elders as to the exact happenings, circumstances, and teachings given through prophetic visions. They did this, of course, to suit their needs and design of control through fear and suppression. Yet we view certain happenings such as the changes in the Earth's vibratory awakening as prophetic accuracy, which was given by those inspired by Spirit.

When you said that those higher energies would cause a breakdown in bodies and minds for those who were ignorant of the higher path of Light, it seems unfair. What about people who are unaware of all that is going on but are really good people?

All are aware within depths of self of this impending transformation taking place. They make their choice by their thoughts, desires, and actions. There is no time to be wishy-washy in your choosing because much is being held in the balance. Daily, the energies increase and intensify in matter manifestation. Those beings who are outwardly unaware are truly inwardly choosing. All beings shall choose as they deem fit for their soul destiny. Higher powers and forces are doing all that is within their means to inform and convince all of their responsibility to themselves, their evolution, and the evolution of this plane. Our purpose is united in this task, and the forces of Light are beckoning to all at this time to come home to their God-self connection through Love, Light, and harmony. That is why your voice and the voices of others are so important at this time to spread the word of Light, using all methods and means possible to help ease this transitional process and inform all who are ready to listen to truths which the Spirit is quickening within mankind's consciousness.

How may we better prepare for these incoming Light energies so that our bodies and minds will not break down?

As the accelerated energies infuse and interpenetrate material form, they bring with them all that is positive, loving, and of Divine harmony. Those beings who harbor hatred, greed, or violence in their minds and hearts will fight these energies and will find them disrupting to their bodies and minds, as is occurring at this very moment worldwide.

Those whose inner truth speaks to them of brotherly love, harmony, and balance will find themselves guided, as if by an unseen hand, to those energies and those places of safety for their own survival within form. They shall blend with the higher energies and expand and flow with the God-force within as it awakens them. That is truly what these energies of Light are. They are energies of awakening and of enlightenment. Yet, to those who love the darkness, they are as enemies to be done away with. Light is always the conqueror of darkness. Those forces of lower density shall be transformed, or they shall perish in the process. On the inner planes, the Forces of Light have already won. As above, so below, and the battle for Light, harmony, and goodness is being enacted now upon the material plane.

Fear not, however, for the Light is assured its place and shall overcome even the most dense of lower energies. It shall be the victor as mankind transforms into God-man and takes his place in the cosmos as heir to the Kingdom of God on Earth. So be it.

It is hard to understand that when we have bills, debts, and responsibilities to meet, we should not worry or feel trapped in the vicious

cycle of making a living to keep going and insure our survival. How realistically can we just "be"? What happens when we don't have rent money, or they take away our car because we cannot make the payments?

Your social structure has set it up so your slavery in mind and body would be assured as your desire and need for possessions and a "quality of life" could be maintained. We are not suggesting that you give up your jobs or sustenance and merely sit upon your bed waiting for the world to hand you your dinner. What we are saying is that the gentler way of being and living is present before you now through the trust in your inner power and strength, and in God's plan for a truly finer quality of life.

Quality of life is not to be found within the acquisition of possessions such as a fine house or car or debts that enslave your mind through worry and stress. Quality of life is found within you in the Love which you share with one another, with the priority of life which you gather unto your experiences through lovingness to yourself and all with whom you come in contact. Quality of life is that which is seen as true freedom from all things which would take away your power and your peace of mind. Quality of life is that soft perception in the foreverness of your being, wherein you know you are beyond all manifest limitation and are owned by no one and no thing.

Quality of life points the path to liberation for it supports the knowledge that all is God and therefore has an equal share and worth in the purpose and plan of unfolding awareness within each consciousness. Truly, the person who owns nothing is at times more at peace than the power-driven man of greed who strives to own the world through manipulation and obsessive behavior.

The power-driven man has many more distractions that keep him from viewing the source of his existence. The person of few possessions, however, has fewer obstacles preventing him from witnessing his own truth. We are not suggesting that one must renounce all possessions in order to find God, but we are saying that priorities of the "quality of living" must be examined and assessed in order to realize a gentler way of perceiving the purpose and worth of one's life and plan.

True wealth is not found through one's bank account, just as true wisdom cannot be measured by the number of university degrees one has. Some of the wisest men do not know how to spell their names, and yet they see beyond this temporal world and move though dimensions of Light and Love which are greater than you can imagine.

Your social structure sets up a great many characteristics which define the term "successful" or one to whom is due honor; yet, it completely neglects and turns its back upon those whose eyes truly see and whose ears truly hear.

That is why each must choose for himself the style or quality of life he wants to lead that will produce peace and happiness while honoring the Earth Mother. Many in your society are now looking upon their lives, wondering how they have become so fearful and overwhelmed by debt. They wonder why they are unhappy in their lives, unfulfilled in their work or careers. They are seeking alternative ways to live without the structured rigidity which has been their lot all these years. They seek a gentler way but do not know how to find it or what steps to take to free themselves. Many of them bring illness or even death into their lives as a means of escape for they feel there is no other way out. It is unfortunate that fear motivation is so ingrained into social behavior that some feel that death is the only way out of one's unhappy or frustrating life. Truly, man was meant to be free, inwardly and outwardly; yet he has been trained since youth in beliefs of enslavement for the purposes of the social hierarchy.

In your country of America, the forefathers, impelled by spiritual understanding, intended and directed this to be a free nation, yet are you truly free if you live in fear? Are you free when your stress-filled mind prevents you from acknowledging your own power? Are you free when your attachment and desire for possessions of this or that rule your life and choice? Are you free when you are judged by your neighbors because of your color or wealth, and that judgment disturbs or concerns you? Are you free when your path is determined by the concepts of others of you instead of by your own concept of yourself?

No, you are not free! You are a slave to the system which governs your steps and converts your free will, directing it in ways which do not serve your soul. In the end, when you lie upon the bed of death, surrounded by your beautiful house and fine possessions, with stacks of money lying beside you on your bed, you shall look upon your life and the struggle for the achievement of possessions and shall realize the futility of it all.

Your journey past death's door shall not be put off one moment longer because of your fortune or fame. What is the true purpose of life if it is lived in the fear of losing that which you have never truly owned in the first place? You cannot even own your own body for it is loaned to you for the gaining of experience. When it is time to return to your Source, it is given up. There is much fuss and bother about which clothes to put on it, which makeup to use to better its appearance. What do all these things really matter in the greater picture? It is true that your body is your temple, but it is not the end-all or the be-all of life. Life is the end-all, the be-all of Life. Life!! What is life if it is lived in fear of survival, in fear of not having enough to pay one's rent, or in fear of this or that?

Enough of this! You are God!

Those who are of the new order shall be those who have let go of fear and struggle. Those who trust in the moment to meet all their needs shall receive, through their faith, all things necessary as they flow with life's current and joy, loving themselves and each other while they ride the winds of change.

THE PATH

Past distant thundering silence,
through gates worn thin from time,
lies a path beyond the shadows' edge,
a land beyond the mind.

There are no signs to point the way,
that road ye walk alone.
Thy feet must step out on the ledge,
perchance to take thee home.
This path its mystery to be found
within a twinkling eye.
Perhaps a smile, a tender glance
shall lead thee by and by.
Down through dark forest,
fearful tears of past belief and thought.
Unspoken grace this magical dance
both kings and beggars sought.
Yet, none has passed on through those gates
with selfish greed at heart.
None save those simple, happy fools
do gain entry by Love's art.
Beyond the bounds of fear and doubt,
this land of peace abides.
The self supreme is he who calls
the reigning king so wise.
Until ye walk this hallowed ground,
thy life is but illusion,
and all ye do and say is done
within the mind's confusion.
To know thyself so near to thee
takes but thy heart's desire.
Thy wish fulfilled, this glowing son
shall lead thee ever higher.
To break the spell, to set thee free,
Light calls out from within.
Awake! Awake, oh, sleeping one,
arise and let Love in.

—Jonathon of the Seventh Ray — May 20, 1991

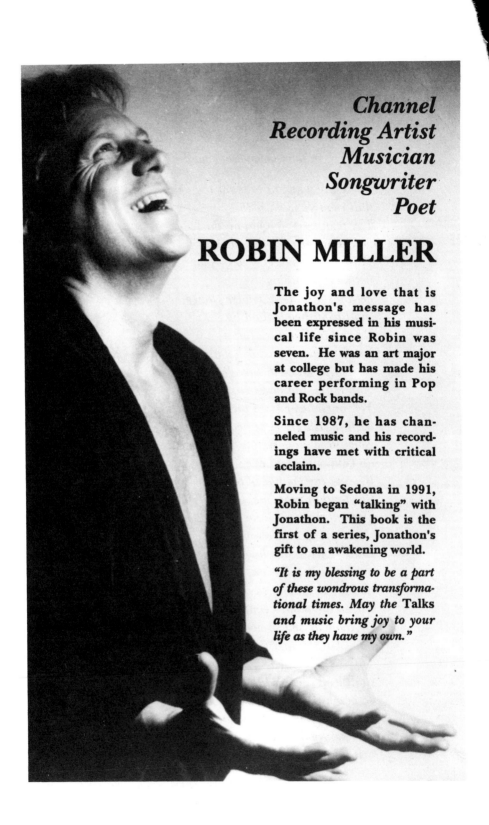

Channel
Recording Artist
Musician
Songwriter
Poet

ROBIN MILLER

The joy and love that is Jonathon's message has been expressed in his musical life since Robin was seven. He was an art major at college but has made his career performing in Pop and Rock bands.

Since 1987, he has channeled music and his recordings have met with critical acclaim.

Moving to Sedona in 1991, Robin began "talking" with Jonathon. This book is the first of a series, Jonathon's gift to an awakening world.

"It is my blessing to be a part of these wondrous transformational times. May the Talks and music bring joy to your life as they have my own."